People, Places, and Things 2

Reading • Vocabulary • Test Preparation

Lin Lougheed

OXFORD
UNIVERSITY PRESS

198 Madison Avenue
New York, NY 10016 USA

Great Clarendon Street, Oxford OX2 6DP UK

Oxford University Press is a department of the University of Oxford. It furthers the University's objective of excellence in research, scholarship, and education by publishing worldwide in

Oxford New York

Auckland Cape Town Dar es Salaam Hong Kong Karachi Kuala Lumpur Madrid Melbourne Mexico City Nairobi New Delhi Shanghai Taipei Toronto

With offices in

Argentina Austria Brazil Chile Czech Republic France Greece Guatemala Hungary Italy Japan Poland Portugal Singapore South Korea Switzerland Thailand Turkey Ukraine Vietnam

OXFORD and OXFORD ENGLISH are registered trademarks of Oxford University Press

Library of Congress Cataloging-in-Publication Data

Lougheed, Lin, 1946–

People, places, and things : reading, vocabulary, test preparation / Lin Lougheed.

p. cm.

Includes indexes.

ISBN-13: 978-0-19-430201-2 (student bk. : level 2)

ISBN-10: 0-19-430201-6 (student bk. : level 2)

[etc.]

1. English language—Textbooks for foreign speakers. 2. English language—Examinations—Study guides. I. Title.

PE1128.L648 2005

428'.0076–dc22

2005049800

Executive Publisher: Nancy Leonhardt
Senior Acquisitions Editor: Chris Balderston
Editor: Anna Teevan
Assistant Editor: Kate Schubert
Art Director: Maj-Britt Hagsted
Senior Designer: Mia Gomez
Art Editor: Robin Fadool
Production Manager: Shanta Persaud
Production Controller: Eve Wong

Additional realia by Mia Gomez

ISBN-13: 978 0 19 430201 2
ISBN-10: 0 19 430201 6

10 9 8 7 6 5 4 3 2 1

Printed in Hong Kong.

Acknowledgments:

Cover photographs: Lee Young-Pyo: AP Photo/Hussein Malla; Mount Lhotse and Mount Everest: ©Brad Wrobleski/Masterfile; Stonehenge: ©SuperStock/Alamy; Chinese Dragon: ©ImageState/Alamy; Tropical fish: ©ImageState/Alamy; Midori Ito: ©Neal Preston/CORBIS.

We would like to thank the following for their permission to reproduce photographs: The Everett Collection p.2; Carolco/The Kobal Collection p.4; Universal/The Kobal Collection p.6; Images.com/Corbis/Phil Bliss/Jim Bliss p.12; National Geographic/Getty Images/George Grall p.14; Corbis/D. Swallow/M. Deutsch/H. Cassea/Gui p.16; Dance Picture Library/photographersdirect.com/ Linda Rich p.22; Associated Press, AP/Stuart Ramson p.24; Dance Picture Library/photographersdirect.com/Linda Rich p.26; Graeme Teague p.32; Getty/Photographer's Choice/Jeff Hunter p.34; Oceanwide Images/Gary Bell p.36; Associated Press, AP/Joe Cavaretta p.42; The Image Bank/Getty/Ryan McVay p.44; Corbis/Earl & Nazima Kowall p.46; The Everett Collection p.52; Robertstock.com/AN2/Popperfoto p.54; Corbis/Coco Masuda p.56; Associated Press, AP/Gail Oskin p.62; Corbis/Henny Abrams p.64; Wolfgang Kaehler p.66; Michael Hortens p.72; Reuters/Corbis/Mike Segar p.74; Corbis/Gareth Brown p.76.

CONTENTS

TO THE TEACHER iv

UNIT 1: STUNTS 2

People: Michelle Yeoh **2**
Places: Stunt Schools **4**
Things: Movie Stunts **6**

UNIT 2: COLOR 12

People: People Who Hear Color **12**
Places: The Amazon Rainforest **14**
Things: Color and Mood **16**

UNIT 3: CIRCUS 22

People: Wayne Huey of the Red Panda Acrobats **22**
Places: The Circus Train **24**
Things: The Chinese Circus **26**

UNIT 4: SHARKS 32

People: Eugenie Clark, the Shark Lady **32**
Places: The Great Barrier Reef **34**
Things: Great White Sharks **36**

UNIT 5: SPORTS 42

People: Se Ri Pak **42**
Places: Sea and Sky **44**
Things: Tae Kwon Do Belts and Uniforms **46**

UNIT 6: MONSTERS 52

People: Count Dracula **52**
Places: Loch Ness and Its Monster **54**
Things: Dragons **56**

UNIT 7: MUSIC 62

People: Han-na Chang **62**
Places: Carnegie Hall **64**
Things: A Stolen Cello **66**

UNIT 8: NEW YEAR 72

People: The Chinese Horoscope and Your Personality **72**
Places: New Year's Eve in Times Square **74**
Things: Celebrating the New Year **76**

Vocabulary Self-Quiz **82**

Vocabulary Index **90**

Common Irregular Verbs **92**

TO THE TEACHER

Welcome to *People, Places, and Things.*

What is in each unit?

Prepare to Read

This section introduces the topic of the passage. The questions encourage students to share their own thoughts and experiences, and can be used for discussion before reading.

Word Focus

This matching activity introduces students to new or unfamiliar words that they will see in the reading passage. Students match the ten words with simple definitions.

Scan

This activity encourages students to make a prediction about a specific piece of information that appears in the passage. The aim is to motivate students to read the passages quickly as they try to find the answer.

Reading Passage

Each reading passage in Book 2 is about 250 words. The eight units each contain three reading passages based around a common theme: the first passage is about a person, the second is about a place, and the third is about a thing. Each reading passage recycles new words from earlier passages so that students can gradually build on and consolidate their vocabulary. The language is carefully graded so that students gain confidence in reading. Each reading passage is also available on an audio CD, narrated by a native English speaker. The CD is available separately.

Which Meaning?

This feature focuses on a word in the passage that has more than one dictionary meaning. Students must choose which of the dictionary definitions fits the word as it is used in the context of the passage. The aim is to encourage students to use dictionaries more effectively, and to think about the meaning of words in context.

Check Your Comprehension

These multiple-choice questions check students' understanding of the passage. The questions include key skills such as understanding the main idea, reading for details, reading for inference, and understanding text references.

Vocabulary Review

This section reviews the vocabulary presented in the unit. It includes a wide variety of activities, such as Words in Context (filling in the gaps), Sentence Completion (completing short advertisements and e-mails), and Wrong Word (finding the word that doesn't fit the group). Other activities include Word Families, Synonyms and Antonyms, True or False, and puzzles such as Crosswords, Word Searches, and Mystery Phrases. The aim is to help students begin to use the new words as part of their active vocabulary.

What About You?

This section is divided into two parts: Speaking and Writing. The aim is to encourage students to use some of the new words they have learned in a more personal context. The activity can be done in pairs or in small groups.

Reading Quiz

This features a short passage—an e-mail, a letter, or a short information piece—followed by six multiple choice test questions. The passage includes many of the new words from the unit. The multiple choice format and the range of question types reflect the style of questions that students will encounter in standardized tests such as the TOIEC® and TOEFL® tests. The aim of the quiz is to act as a unit test, and also to help students with test preparation.

Extra Features

Vocabulary Self-Quiz

This is a unit-by-unit word list which lists the new words in each passage. There is a space next to each word where students can write a translation, or other notes, and there is also a space for them to test themselves. The aim is to help students study and review the words outside class.

Vocabulary Index

This is an index of the new vocabulary items which appear in the passages. Each item is followed by a reference to the passage where it is introduced, and also to the subsequent passages where it reappears.

Answer Key

The Answer Key is available on the OUP Website, and can be downloaded at www.oup.com/elt/teacher/peopleplacesandthings.

ACKNOWLEDGMENTS

The author and publisher would like to thank the following teachers, whose reviews, comments, and suggestions contributed to the development of *People, Places, and Things*:

Jeong Mi Choi, BCM Junior High School, Seoul, Korea; Jeremy Greenway, Shinmin Senior High School, Taichung, Taiwan; Sabrina Hsieh, Sacred Heart High School, Touliu, Taiwan; Shigeru Ichikawa, Todaiji Gakuen Junior and Senior High Schools, Nara, Japan; Tae Woo Kang, Kang Tae Woo Language School, Seoul, Korea; Josie Lai, Hsin Sheng Children's English School, Taoyuan, Taiwan; Jessie Lee, Tunghai University, Taichung, Taiwan; Masahiro Shirai, Doshisha Girls' Junior and Senior High Schools, Kyoto, Japan; Atsuko Tsuda, Keio Gijuku University, Tokyo, Japan; Arthur Tu, Taipei YMCA, Taipei, Taiwan.

In addition, the author would like to thank the following for their helpful comments and suggestions: Richard Firsten, Lindsey Hopkins Technical Education Center, Miami, Florida, U.S.A.; Maureen McCarthy, Miami Dade College, Miami, Florida, U.S.A.; Christine Meloni, Ph.D., George Washington University, Washington, DC, U.S.A.; Maureen O'Hara, Miami Dade College, Miami, Florida, U.S.A.; Katherine Rawson, Montgomery College, Montgomery County, Maryland, U.S.A.; Cynthia Schuemann, Miami Dade College, Miami, Florida, U.S.A.

UNIT 1

STUNTS

PEOPLE

Michelle Yeoh

PREPARE TO READ

Discuss these questions.

1. What do you know about Michelle Yeoh?
2. Would you like to have a job like hers? Why or why not?

WORD FOCUS

Match the words with their definitions.

A.

1. contest __	a. hurt
2. dream __	b. in place of
3. fascinate __	c. interest strongly
4. injure __	d. a competition
5. instead __	e. think about something you want

B.

1. kick __	a. have an important part in a movie
2. punch __	b. hit with the foot
3. star __	c. a person between the ages of 13 and 19
4. stunt __	d. a difficult physical trick
5. teenager __	e. hit with the hand

SCAN

A. Guess the answer. Circle *a* or *b*.
Where is Michelle Yeoh from?

a. California ***b.*** Malaysia

B. Scan the passage quickly to check your answer.

TRACK 2

Michelle Yeoh

When Michelle Yeoh was a girl, she **dreamed** of being a dancer. Later on, she became a beauty queen. But she isn't famous for these things. She is famous for her amazing work in movies as an actress and **stunt** performer.

Michelle Yeoh was born in Malaysia. As a young girl she enjoyed sports, especially swimming. She liked music and art, too, but she loved dance the most. As a **teenager**, she went to England to study dance. While studying dance, she **injured** her back. That's when she started studying acting **instead**.

After Yeoh went back home, she participated in a beauty **contest**. She won and became Miss Malaysia. Soon after that, she went to Hong Kong to become an actress. While she worked in the movies, she watched the stunt actors. She decided that she wanted to do stunts, too. She spent hours every day at the gym. She learned how to **punch** and **kick**. She started doing her own stunts in the movies.

Yeoh **starred** in her first movie in 1979. In her movies, she does most of her own stunts. In one movie, she rode a motorcycle along the roof of a moving train. In another, she jumped off a bridge and onto a moving truck. She became famous around the world when she starred in *Tomorrow Never Dies* with Pierce Brosnan. In 2000, she starred in *Crouching Tiger, Hidden Dragon*.

Michelle Yeoh is one of the most famous stunt actors in the world. Her amazing stunts **fascinate** people everywhere.

WHICH MEANING?
What does *back* mean in line 7?

1 (*preposition*) behind
2 (*verb*) move backwards
3 (*noun*) a part of the body

CHECK YOUR COMPREHENSION

Read the passage again and answer the questions. Circle your answers.

MAIN IDEA

1. What is this passage mainly about?

A. Hong Kong movies
B. A beauty contest
C. A movie actress
D. Pierce Brosnan

DETAIL

2. What did Michelle Yeoh study in England?

A. Sports
B. Stunts
C. Music and art
D. Dance and acting

3. Which sport did Yeoh like the most when she was young?

A. Gymnastics
B. Swimming
C. Kickboxing
D. Jumping

4. What did Yeoh do in 1979?

A. She won a beauty contest.
B. She acted in a movie.
C. She jumped off a bridge.
D. She hurt her back.

INFERENCE

5. Why did Yeoh stop studying dance?

A. Dance lessons were too expensive.
B. Her real dream was to be a movie star.
C. Her parents wanted her to be an actress.
D. She couldn't dance with an injured back.

TEXT REFERENCE

6. In line 15, *In another, she jumped off a bridge*, what does the word *another* refer to?

A. A train
B. A movie
C. An actor
D. A motorcycle

PLACES

PREPARE TO READ

Discuss these questions.

1. Describe a movie stunt that you remember.
2. How do people learn to do movie stunts?

WORD FOCUS

Match the words with their definitions.

A.

1. acrobatics __	a. a class
2. applicant __	b. sign up for a class
3. course __	c. a person who applies to enter a school
4. enroll __	d. sports such as karate, tae kwon do, etc.
5. martial arts __	e. a sport that involves amazing bending, balancing, and jumping

B.

1. mentally __	a. related to the body
2. physically __	b. make necessary
3. require __	c. pants
4. train __	d. related to the mind
5. trousers __	e. learn or teach

SCAN

A. Guess the answer. Circle *a* or *b*.

Jackie Chan went to stunt school in

a. Hong Kong. ***b.*** Korea.

B. Scan the passage quickly to check your answer.

TRACK 3 

Stunt Schools

Where do you go to become a stunt actor? Jackie Chan went to the China Drama Academy in Hong Kong. Every day from 5 A.M. to midnight, he and his classmates studied singing, **acrobatics**, gymnastics, and **martial arts**. They started at a young age and lived at the school. Jackie Chan lived at the school for ten years. The students at the China Drama Academy were very strong and very well **trained**. Many stunt actors came from this school. They were called Red Trousers because the students were **required** to wear red **trousers** at school.

There are other training centers, such as the Seoul Action School in Korea, where you don't have to **enroll** at such a young age. At this school, you can learn everything from basic gymnastics and martial arts to stunt driving in six months. Many students don't finish. The **courses** are very difficult both **mentally** and **physically**.

Applicants to the Seoul Action School must be between 19 and 27 years old, at least 170 centimeters tall, and must look good in films. The teachers at the Seoul Action School work in Korean films and know all about martial arts as well as Hollywood-style car chases and crashes.

If you have less time, you can take a three-week course at the International Stunt School in Seattle. In three weeks, you will learn basic fire and driving stunts, gymnastics, and high falls. If you are really short on time, you can even take a stunt course by mail!

WHICH MEANING?

What does *age* mean in line 7?

1 (*verb*) become older
2 (*noun*) the number of years you have lived
3 (*noun*) an important period in history

CHECK YOUR COMPREHENSION

Read the passage again and answer the questions. Circle your answers.

MAIN IDEA

1. What is this passage mainly about?

A. The China Drama Academy
B. Different stunt schools
C. Famous stunt actors
D. Korean films

DETAIL

2. How long was Jackie Chan a student at the China Drama Academy?

A. Three weeks
B. Six months
C. Five years
D. Ten years

3. What is one thing you cannot study at the Seoul Action School?

A. Singing
B. Martial arts
C. Gymnastics
D. Stunt driving

4. Where is the International Stunt School?

A. Hong Kong
B. Korea
C. Seattle
D. Seoul

INFERENCE

5. Why did Jackie Chan live at the China Drama Academy?

A. He had to study longer than the other students.
B. The academy was very far from his house.
C. All the academy students lived there.
D. He didn't have his own home.

TEXT ORGANIZATION

6. Which paragraph mentions requirements for becoming a student at the Seoul Action School?

A. The first paragraph
B. The second paragraph
C. The third paragraph
D. The fourth paragraph

THINGS

PREPARE TO READ

Discuss these questions.

1. What are some things that stunt actors have to do?
2. How do stunt actors stay safe while doing stunts?

WORD FOCUS

Match the words with their definitions.

A.

1. audience __	a. not afraid
2. brave __	b. act as if something is true
3. explode __	c. fire
4. flame __	d. blow up like a bomb
5. pretend __	e. the people who watch a performance

B.

1. protect __	a. dangerous
2. risky __	b. turn upside down
3. shoot __	c. keep safe
4. spin __	d. use a gun
5. turn over __	e. turn around very quickly

SCAN

A. Guess the answer. Circle *a* or *b*.

When a stunt actor jumps from a high place, he usually falls

a. into a pool. ***b.*** onto an airbag.

B. Scan the passage quickly to check your answer.

TRACK 4

MOVIE STUNTS A stunt actor's job looks exciting, but it is often difficult and dangerous. Stunt actors jump off high buildings, fall off mountains, get shot, crash cars, or catch on fire. They need special training to do these stunts safely, and they need good acting skills to make the stunts look real.

Stunt actors have to know different punches and kicks for stunt fighting. They have to make the **audience** believe the fight is a real fight. If they receive a punch or a kick, they have to make the pain look real.

Sometimes stunt actors have to fall or jump from very high places. They usually fall onto an airbag, but while they fall they have to act. For example, maybe someone **shoots** the character while he is falling. The stunt actor has to **pretend** he is really in pain.

Stunt actors often have to do driving stunts like making the car **spin** around, **turn over**, and finally crash. Then they have to run away from the burning car before it **explodes**.

Fire stunts are very **risky**. Stunt actors use real fire. Even though they use fire suits, gloves, powder, and other things to **protect** themselves during fire stunts, the **flames** are still hot.

Of course, stunts aren't real, but they are still risky. Stunt actors have to look injured. At the same time, they have to protect themselves from really being injured. You need a lot of skill to do stunts. You also need to be **brave**.

WHICH MEANING?
What does *character* mean in line 10?

1 (*noun*) a person in a book or movie
2 (*noun*) a Chinese letter
3 (*noun*) personality

CHECK YOUR COMPREHENSION

Read the passage again and answer the questions. Circle your answers.

MAIN IDEA

1. What is this passage mainly about?

A. How to become a stunt actor
B. Safety while doing stunts
C. Learning stunt skills
D. A stunt actor's job

DETAIL

2. What skills does a stunt actor need?

A. Acting
B. Driving
C. Punching and kicking
D. All of the above

3. Stunt actors use ________ to protect themselves during fire stunts.

A. airbags
B. powder
C. water
D. cars

4. Which of the following is NOT true?

A. Actors use real fire during fire stunts.
B. Most stunts are not really dangerous.
C. Stunt actors pretend to feel pain.
D. A stunt fight looks real to the audience.

INFERENCE

5. What is a fire suit?

A. Clothes that don't burn easily
B. A uniform for a fire fighter
C. Clothes the color of fire
D. A very warm suit

TEXT ORGANIZATION

6. Which paragraph mentions fighting stunts?

A. The first paragraph
B. The second paragraph
C. The third paragraph
D. The fourth paragraph

VOCABULARY REVIEW

WORD SEARCH

Find and circle the vocabulary below. Then look for the hidden message formed by unused letters in the first three lines of the puzzle.

- contest
- fascinate
- physically
- audience
- risky
- shoot
- spin
- protect
- brave
- applicant

J	A	C	K	I	Y	C	O	N	T	E	S	T	E	F
C	H	A	N	W	L	K	O	R	E	R	E	D	A	B
T	E	R	O	U	L	S	S	E	R	S	T	S	R	E
M	C	Q	B	I	A	H	O	I	Z	K	C	A	R	S
B	N	Y	Z	J	C	P	C	L	R	I	V	M	A	Q
O	E	D	N	N	I	P	S	A	N	E	W	C	B	O
D	I	W	H	G	S	I	Z	A	D	I	J	G	K	O
U	D	Q	O	O	Y	U	T	C	A	D	N	U	K	K
M	U	T	I	S	H	E	M	E	D	B	K	V	E	N
T	A	W	A	T	P	T	N	A	C	I	L	P	P	A
T	C	E	T	O	R	P	S	Y	N	J	J	G	U	R
P	O	F	K	O	Y	H	I	M	J	A	W	U	Q	R
S	F	V	D	H	O	R	E	H	M	R	E	G	E	Y
O	O	E	S	S	H	R	C	F	G	L	A	F	D	L

Hidden message:

☐☐☐☐☐☐ ☐☐☐☐ ☐☐☐☐ ☐☐☐ ☐☐☐☐☐☐☐☐.

WORDS IN CONTEXT

Fill in the blanks with words from each box.

mentally	pretended	turned over	starred	instead

1. The car _______ in the accident, but no one was hurt.
2. Jackie Chan has _______ in many action movies.
3. The actress didn't really feel cold; she just _______.
4. I don't want to go to the movies tonight. I think I'll watch TV _______.
5. Stunts are both physically and _______ difficult. They challenge body and mind.

stunt	martial arts	age	flame	character

6. In this movie, one _______ drives her car off a bridge.
7. _______ such as karate and judo are very popular these days.
8. Michelle Yeoh learned to swim at a young _______.
9. Jumping from a tall building onto an airbag is a difficult _______ to do.
10. A candle _______ is hot, but it doesn't provide much light.

kick	injure	require	enroll	dream

11. A good soccer player can _______ the ball far.
12. I _______ of becoming a stunt actor like Jackie Chan.
13. If you want to learn to do stunts, you can _______ in a stunt school.
14. The stunt actor crashed the car, but she didn't _______ herself.
15. Our teachers _______ us to do homework every day.

WORD FAMILIES

Fill in the blanks with words from each box.

trainer (*noun*)	**training** (*noun*)	**train** (*verb*)

1. Good _______ is very important for stunt actors.
2. A stunt actor has to _______ every day.

acrobat (*noun*)	**acrobatics** (*noun*)	**acrobatic** (*adjective*)

3. The _______ stood on his hands and walked across the room.
4. It isn't easy to learn to do _______.

explosion (*noun*)	**exploded** (*verb*)	**explosive** (*adjective*)

5. When the car hit the bridge, it _______.
6. We could hear the _______ from far away.

WRONG WORD

One word in each group does not fit. Circle the word.

1. back	arm	down	neck
2. hit	carry	punch	kick
3. teacher	teenager	baby	adult
4. course	school	study	sleep
5. pants	shorts	trousers	sweater
6. martial arts	mathematics	gymnastics	acrobatics

SENTENCE COMPLETION

Complete the advertisement with words from the box.

enroll	courses	train	martial arts	teenagers

Learn stunts at the National Stunt School.

- We will _______ you to do amazing stunts, just like in the movies.
- We also have _______ in gymnastics, acrobatics, and _______.
- We have classes for all ages—children, _______, and adults.
- *Don't wait! Call or visit the school today to _______ in classes.*

WHAT ABOUT YOU?

Speaking

Ask your partner these questions.

1. What do you dream of doing in the future?
2. Which is your favorite course in school this year?
3. At what age did you learn to read?
4. Which actors star in your favorite movie?
5. What kind of contest would you like to enter? Why?

Writing

Now write about your partner. Use your partner's answers to the questions.

Example: Mary dreams of traveling around the world in the future.

1. ______________________________
2. ______________________________
3. ______________________________
4. ______________________________
5. ______________________________

READING QUIZ

Read the passage and answer the questions. Circle your answers.

Kicks for Kids

Do you dream of being a stunt actor like Jackie Chan or Michelle Yeoh? Are you tired of always sitting in the audience watching others living your dream? If you answered "Yes!" to these questions, and you are a teenager between the ages of 14 and 18, we want to hear from you. Don't wait for the next new stunt actor to fascinate you. Learn how to make your own dreams come true. In just 12 weeks, we will give you the many skills that you need to become a stunt actor.

Our stunt school will:

- train you to kick, spin, and punch*
- train you mentally and physically
- train you in acrobatics
- train you to protect yourself in a real fire or explosion

Enroll in our special course for teens today. The first twenty applicants will be part of our special contest. You could star in a TV ad for our school! Call today: 333-KICK.

*At our school we train people to pretend. This is not a martial arts school. However, stunt acting is risky. You could get injured. We require parents to be at the first Kicks for Kids meeting.

MAIN IDEA

1. What is this advertisement for?

A. A movie starring Jackie Chan and Michelle Yeoh
B. A chance to meet famous actors
C. A stunt school for teenagers
D. A martial arts class

DETAIL

2. What age are the youngest participants in Kicks for Kids?

A. 12 years old
B. 13 years old
C. 14 years old
D. 18 years old

3. Who has to attend the first Kicks for Kids meeting?

A. Parents
B. Acrobats
C. Stunt Actors
D. Martial arts teachers

INFERENCE

4. Who will star in a TV ad?

A. The first twenty applicants
B. The contest winner
C. Parents of teens
D. Jackie Chan

VOCABULARY

5. What does *dream* in line 1 mean?

A. Sleep
B. Watch movies
C. Think about
D. Tell stories

6. What does *risky* in line 27 mean?

A. Exciting
B. Expensive
C. Interesting
D. Dangerous

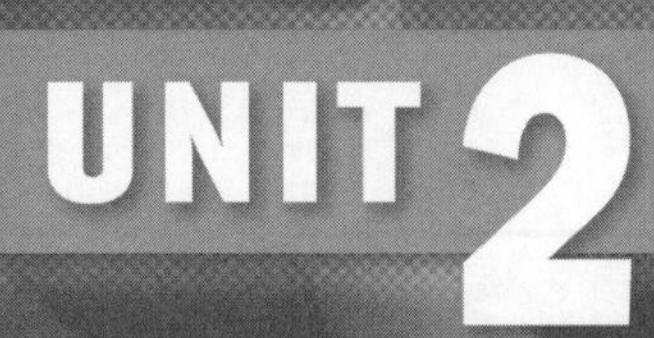

COLOR

PEOPLE

PREPARE TO READ

Discuss these questions.

1. Think about the room around you. What are some things you can see, hear, feel, and smell?
2. In what activities do you use two or more senses at the same time?

WORD FOCUS

Match the words with their definitions.

A.

1. colorful __	**a.** a type or kind
2. condition __	**b.** give information
3. experience __	**c.** a way of being
4. form __	**d.** full of color
5. report __	**e.** do or feel something

B.

1. sense __	**a.** not together
2. separate __	**b.** a shape with three sides
3. smooth __	**c.** the ability to see, hear, taste, smell, or feel
4. strange __	**d.** unusual
5. triangle __	**e.** flat; without bumps

SCAN

A. Guess the answer. Circle *a* or *b*.

When a person experiences two senses at the same time, this is called

a. synesthesia. ***b.*** double senses.

B. Scan the passage quickly to check your answer.

TRACK 5

People Who Hear Color

What color is your name? What color is Wednesday? These questions might <u>sound</u> **strange** to most people, but some can answer right away. One person says her name is the color red. For another person, Wednesday is blue. These people have a **condition** called *synesthesia*. This means they **experience** two **senses** at the same time. For these people, the senses of smell, sound, sight, touch, and taste are not **separate**. They might see and also hear colors, for example, or hear as well as feel sounds.

The most frequent **form** of synesthesia is to hear sounds as colors. A person with synesthesia might hear the number three as blue or the letter *D* as red. Someone might always see green upon hearing the word *April*. Another person might see different colors while listening to music. Some people also taste colors. To one person, a steak might taste blue and to another, yellow. Some people experience feelings in color. For example, one person with synesthesia **reports** feeling pain as the color orange.

Another form of synesthesia is to experience sounds or tastes as shapes. Some people see music as **triangles** and circles. Some people taste mint as a **smooth** ball. There are other forms of synesthesia, as well. For one man, different words have different tastes. Some words taste like bacon; others taste like potatoes or eggs.

Synesthesia is not a common condition. Perhaps only one person in every 5,000 has it. For these people, the everyday world can be a **colorful** and fascinating place.

WHICH MEANING?
What does *sound* mean in line 2?

1 (*noun*) noise
2 (*adjective*) healthy
3 (*verb*) seem

CHECK YOUR COMPREHENSION

Read the passage again and answer the questions. Circle your answers.

MAIN IDEA

1. What is this passage mainly about?

A. An unusual condition
B. People who like color
C. The color of pain
D. Music and art

DETAIL

2. Which statement is true about people with synesthesia?

A. They don't see well.
B. They might hear sounds as colors.
C. They usually like the taste of bacon.
D. They always see Wednesday as blue.

3. Which is the most common form of synesthesia?

A. Experiencing taste as shapes
B. Experiencing sound as color
C. Experiencing words as taste
D. Experiencing music as shapes

4. How many people probably have synesthesia?

A. Only 5,000 in the world
B. One out of every 500
C. About 5 million
D. One out of every 5,000

INFERENCE

5. Which of the following is NOT an example of synesthesia?

A. Feeling pain in red
B. Tasting steak as green
C. Feeling warm in April
D. Seeing music as squares

TEXT ORGANIZATION

6. Which paragraph mentions tasting shapes?

A. The first paragraph
B. The second paragraph
C. The third paragraph
D. The fourth paragraph

PLACES

poison arrow frog

PREPARE TO READ

Discuss these questions.

1. What do you know about animals in the Amazon rainforest?
2. What are some ways that color is very important for animals?

WORD FOCUS

Match the words with their definitions.

A.

1. bright __	**a.** strong in color
2. death __	**b.** weak in color
3. dull __	**c.** a type of lizard
4. grab __	**d.** take quickly
5. iguana __	**e.** a noun for *die*

B.

1. poison __	**a.** tell about danger
2. predator __	**b.** hold very tightly
3. prey __	**c.** an animal that hunts
4. squeeze __	**d.** an animal that other animals hunt
5. warn __	**e.** material that can kill people or animals

SCAN

A. Guess the answer. Circle *a* or *b*.

What color are some boa constrictor snakes?

a. Gray or brown   *b.* Orange or red

B. Scan the passage quickly to check your answer.

TRACK 6

The Amazon Rainforest

There are thousands of species of animals in the Amazon rainforest, each colored differently. Most rainforest animals use their colors for survival.

Some animals use color to protect themselves from their **predators**. An example is the green **iguana**. Young iguanas are **bright** green and hide among the bright green lower leaves of the trees where they live. As they get older, their color becomes **duller**. Older iguanas live higher in the trees, where the colors all around are less bright.

Other animals are predators and use color to hide from their **prey**. The boa constrictor snake is a good example. Some boas are gray or brown, and these colors help them hide on branches. The emerald boa is green and white, so it can easily hide in the leaves. A boa hides in a tree and waits for a bird to fly by. When one does, the boa **grabs** the bird from the air and then **squeezes** it to **death** before eating it.

Poison arrow frogs don't try to hide. They want everyone to see them. These colorful frogs can be orange, red, or green. Their bright colors let everybody know where they are. The bright color **warns** other animals that the frog is poisonous, so they stay away. These tiny frogs are very poisonous! One frog has enough poison to kill 100 people.

The colors of the rainforest are beautiful to us, but to the animals they are very important. They help the animals survive.

WHICH MEANING?
What does *fly* mean in line 11?

1 (*verb*) travel through the air
2 (*noun*) a kind of insect
3 (*verb*) escape

CHECK YOUR COMPREHENSION

Read the passage again and answer the questions. Circle your answers.

MAIN IDEA

1. What is this passage mainly about?

A. Predators of the rainforest
B. How rainforest animals live
C. Poisonous rainforest animals
D. How colors protect rainforest animals

DETAIL

2. What color are young iguanas?

A. Dull green
B. Bright green
C. Green and white
D. Orange, red, and green

3. What do boa constrictors eat?

A. Birds
B. Leaves
C. Older iguanas
D. Poison arrow frogs

4. What is true about poison arrow frogs?

A. They like to hide.
B. They are predators.
C. They have bright colors.
D. They aren't very poisonous.

INFERENCE

5. Why might a bird fly near a boa constrictor?

A. Because it moves faster than the boa constrictor
B. Because it isn't afraid of the boa constrictor
C. Because it wants to eat the boa constrictor
D. Because it can't see the boa constrictor

TEXT REFERENCE

6. In line 5, *As they get older, their color becomes duller*, what does the word *they* refer to?

A. Trees
B. Iguanas
C. Leaves
D. Snakes

THINGS

PREPARE TO READ

Discuss these questions.

1. Which colors make you feel happy?
2. Imagine that you could paint your classroom any colors you wanted. Which colors would you choose?

WORD FOCUS

Match the words with their definitions.

A.

1. affect __	**a.** make someone want to do something
2. beige __	**b.** a quiet or peaceful feeling
3. calm __	**c.** make pretty
4. decorate __	**d.** change
5. encourage __	**e.** a very light brown color

B.

1. mood __	**a.** good
2. negative __	**b.** not good
3. positive __	**c.** giving new energy
4. public __	**d.** a feeling
5. refreshing __	**e.** open to everybody; not private

SCAN

A. Guess if this is true or false. Circle *a* or *b*.

Blue is a relaxing color.

a. True ***b.*** False

B. Scan the passage quickly to check your answer.

TRACK 7

Color and Mood

Do some colors make you feel **calm** while others give you energy? Scientists have been studying the connection between color and **mood** for a long time. Many believe that color can **affect** our moods.

Warm, bright colors such as yellow, red, and orange are active colors. They can give people a **positive** feeling, and they **encourage** conversation. Cool colors such as blue, purple, and green are relaxing colors. They help people experience calm feelings.

Many **public** places are **decorated** with certain colors in order to create certain moods. Orange makes people feel hungry, and many restaurants are painted this color. Quiet colors like gray and **beige** are relaxing. These colors are common in doctors' offices and hospitals.

People also use color in their homes to create moods. Warm colors make a room feel warm and comfortable. Yellow is a warm and energizing color. It might be a good color for a kitchen because it can help you wake up during breakfast. Blue is a peaceful color. It helps you rest, so it is a very good color for a bedroom. Green is another good color for a bedroom because it is **refreshing**.

Colors can create **negative** moods, too. Some kinds of blue make people feel sad. Red can give people energy, or it can make people feel angry.

What is your mood right now? Do you feel energized or relaxed, sad or angry? Now look at the color of the walls around you. Does it match your mood?

WHICH MEANING?
What does *make* mean in line 23?

1 (*verb*) create
2 (*verb*) cause
3 (*verb*) earn

CHECK YOUR COMPREHENSION

Read the passage again and answer the questions. Circle your answers.

MAIN IDEA

1. What is this passage mainly about?

A. Good colors for decorating rooms
B. How color affects our feelings
C. How to improve your mood
D. Different ways to relax

DETAIL

2. Which colors make people feel like talking?

A. Yellow and red
B. Blue and green
C. Gray and beige
D. Purple and orange

3. Which statement is true about the color green?

A. It is a warm color.
B. It is an active color.
C. It is a cool color.
D. It is an angry color.

4. Which color is often used in restaurants?

A. Purple
B. Beige
C. Orange
D. Yellow

INFERENCE

5. What is a color you should avoid if you are on a diet?

A. Gray
B. Orange
C. Yellow
D. Beige

TEXT REFERENCE

6. In line 2, *while others give you energy*, what does the word *others* refer to?

A. Scientists
B. Moods
C. People
D. Colors

VOCABULARY REVIEW

CROSSWORD PUZZLE

Complete the crossword using the clues.

Across

3. tell someone to be careful

5. opposite of life

6. take apart or divide

7. not normal

Down

1. strong in color

2. what prey fears

4. a feeling of peace

6. Taste is one type of this.

7. A baby's cheek feels like this.

WORDS IN CONTEXT

Fill in the blanks with words from each box.

refreshing	beige	colorful	mood	smooth

1. The skin of a baby is very _______.

2. A cold drink is _______ on a hot day.

3. People often smile when they are in a good _______.

4. I want to paint this room _______ because I prefer light colors.

5. Rainbows are pretty because they are so _______.

grabbed	warned	reported	experienced	sounded

6. Sam was so hungry that he _______ all the cookies on the plate.

7. When I talked to my friend on the telephone last night, he _______ tired.

8. The car horn _______ us to get out of the way.

9. The newspaper _______ good weather for today.

10. We _______ a lot of interesting things on our trip to the rainforest.

sense	iguanas	condition	makes	affects

11. _______ are beautiful lizards that live in different parts of the world.
12. Green is a color that usually _______ people feel relaxed.
13. Many animals have a very good _______ of smell.
14. Weather _______ my mood, and I usually feel sad on a rainy day.
15. Synesthesia is an unusual and interesting _______.

WORD FAMILIES

Fill in the blanks with words from each box.

poison (*noun*)	**poison** (*verb*)	**poisonous** (*adjective*)

1. Some snakes are very _______; others are not.
2. A snake can _______ you with its bite.

decorations (*noun*)	**decorate** (*verb*)	**decorative** (*adjective*)

3. We like to _______ the house for holidays.
4. We hang _______ both inside and outside the house.

encouragement (*noun*)	**encourage** (*verb*)	**encouraging** (*adjective*)

5. My teacher gave me a lot of _______ and helped me pass the test.
6. The high grade on my test was very _______.

SYNONYMS OR ANTONYMS?

Look at the word pairs. Are the words synonyms, antonyms, or neither? Check the correct answer.

			Synonyms	Antonyms	Neither
1.	bright	dull	☐	☐	☐
2.	smooth	rough	☐	☐	☐
3.	strange	unusual	☐	☐	☐
4.	predator	prey	☐	☐	☐
5.	fly	swim	☐	☐	☐
6.	calm	peaceful	☐	☐	☐
7.	squeeze	hold	☐	☐	☐
8.	triangle	square	☐	☐	☐
9.	colorful	red	☐	☐	☐
10.	positive	negative	☐	☐	☐

		Synonyms	Antonyms	Neither
11. public	private	☐	☐	☐
12. form	type	☐	☐	☐
13. separate	divided	☐	☐	☐
14. grab	take	☐	☐	☐
15. death	life	☐	☐	☐

WHAT ABOUT YOU?

Speaking

Ask your partner these questions.

1. What do your friends encourage you to do?
2. What decorations do you have in your room?
3. What's your mood today?
4. When do you feel calm?
5. Who helps you feel positive?

Writing

Now write about your partner. Use your partner's answers to the questions.

Example: Tom's friends encourage him to play sports.

1. ______________________________
2. ______________________________
3. ______________________________
4. ______________________________
5. ______________________________

READING QUIZ

Read the passage and answer the questions. Circle your answers.

Dreams are difficult to remember. What did you dream last night? Maybe you can't remember your whole dream, but do you remember an object or a place from it? If so, what color was it? Was there a blue car or a white house? Was your mother wearing yellow? Look at the color report to find out what certain colors mean in our dreams.

COLOR REPORT

Blue: This is a positive color. It shows that your life is in order. Like water, blue is calm and refreshing.

Black: This is a negative color. It is sometimes called a non-color. A dream that you remember as black might warn of a death or illness.

Gray: This color means you are experiencing new things. An object that is a dull gray color in your dream means fear.

White: Some dreams are so bright people describe them as white. White objects or places mean hope for the future.

Yellow: Watch for people dressed in yellow in your dreams. They may encourage you to make a big change.

MAIN IDEA

1. What is this passage mainly about?

A. People's favorite colors
B. The meaning of colors
C. Colors for clothes
D. Colors of places

DETAIL

2. Which color means hope for the future?

A. Blue
B. Gray
C. White
D. Yellow

INFERENCE

3. If you dream about ________, something bad might happen to you.

A. a black cat
B. a white house
C. a blue car
D. a yellow dress

TEXT REFERENCE

4. In line 2, *but do you remember an object or a place from it*, what does the word *it* refer to?

A. A color
B. An object
C. A place
D. A dream

VOCABULARY

5. What does *positive* in line 7 mean?

A. Calm
B. Good
C. Pretty
D. Peaceful

6. What does *death* in line 11 mean?

A. Bad health
B. An accident
C. The end of life
D. A serious problem

UNIT 3

CIRCUS

PEOPLE

PREPARE TO READ

Discuss these questions.

1. What are some things that acrobats can do?
2. Look at the acrobats in the picture. What skills do they need to do that trick?

WORD FOCUS

Match the words with their definitions.

A.

1. accomplishment __	a. thinking hard about just one thing
2. balance __	b. reaching a goal
3. concentration __	c. a person born in a particular place
4. juggle __	d. keep from falling down
5. native __	e. throw and catch several small items repeatedly

B.

1. original __	a. first
2. patience __	b. connect
3. perseverance __	c. highly trained; very skilled
4. professional __	d. ability to wait
5. tie in __	e. continuing until you reach your goal

SCAN

A. Guess the answer. Circle *a* or *b*.

How old was Wayne Huey when he began training to be an acrobat?

a. 5 years old ***b.*** 25 years old

B. Scan the passage quickly to check your answer.

TRACK 8

Wayne Huey of the Red Panda Acrobats

"Don't try this at home," Wayne Huey sometimes says to his audience. Then he squeezes himself into a barrel or runs across a room **juggling** bricks. Huey, a **native** of San Francisco, is one of the **original** members of the acrobatic group the Red Pandas. This group performs traditional Chinese acrobatics for schools and businesses all over the world.

Huey always dreamed of becoming a **professional** in Chinese acrobatics. At the age of 25, he enrolled in the Shanghai Circus School. Just being accepted into the school was an **accomplishment**. Most Chinese acrobats begin training as young children, not when they are 25. Huey, whose parents were both born in China, was the first non-native student to be accepted at the world-famous circus school.

The Red Pandas' performances for schoolchildren are both entertaining and educational. Huey teaches the students about Chinese culture and acrobatic history, and he **ties in** the important messages of hard work and **perseverance** as well. He talks about very young kids who train for 40 hours a week in the Chinese circus and then go to school at night.

Wayne Huey says that the key to acrobatics is **concentration**. For example, when he is standing on one hand on a pile of bricks, he only thinks about one thing—being able to **balance**. Huey talks to his audiences about practice, perseverance, and **patience**: the three *P*s which are goals for all of us in our everyday lives.

WHICH MEANING?
What does *key* mean in line 16?

1 (*noun*) the most important point
2 (*noun*) something you use to open a door
3 (*noun*) a musical term

CHECK YOUR COMPREHENSION

Read the passage again and answer the questions. Circle your answers.

MAIN IDEA

1. What is this passage mainly about?
- **A.** The tradition of Chinese acrobatics
- **B.** An acrobat from San Francisco
- **C.** The key to acrobatics
- **D.** Acrobatic training

DETAIL

2. Where do the Red Pandas perform?
- **A.** In China only
- **B.** In circuses
- **C.** In San Francisco only
- **D.** In schools and businesses

3. Who trains for 40 hours a week?
- **A.** Wayne Huey
- **B.** The Red Pandas acrobats
- **C.** Kids in the Chinese circus
- **D.** All acrobats

4. What does Huey think about when he performs acrobatics?
- **A.** The audience
- **B.** Balancing
- **C.** His parents
- **D.** Training

INFERENCE

5. Which of the following do you need to be a good acrobat?
- **A.** Hard work and perseverance
- **B.** Training at a Chinese circus school
- **C.** Knowledge of Chinese culture
- **D.** Experience with the Red Pandas

TEXT ORGANIZATION

6. Which paragraph talks about a circus school?
- **A.** The first paragraph
- **B.** The second paragraph
- **C.** The third paragraph
- **D.** The fourth paragraph

PLACES

PREPARE TO READ

Discuss these questions.

1. Why are these elephants walking through this tunnel?
2. What are some circus animals? How do circus animals usually travel from city to city?

WORD FOCUS

Match the words with their definitions.

A.

1. caretaker __	**a.** move toward
2. coach __	**b.** whole
3. entire __	**c.** things you need to do a job
4. equipment __	**d.** a passenger car on a train
5. head __	**e.** a person who takes care of something

B.

1. load __	**a.** arrive at
2. pull into __	**b.** pack; put on a truck or train
3. snack __	**c.** unpack; take off a truck or train
4. sore __	**d.** painful
5. unload __	**e.** a small meal

SCAN

A. Guess the answer. Circle *a* or *b*.

How long is the Ringling Brothers and Barnum and Bailey Circus train?

a. 3.2 kilometers ***b.*** 32 cars

B. Scan the passage quickly to check your answer.

TRACK 9

The Circus Train

A circus train is very much like a small town. For much of the year, the Ringling Brothers and Barnum and Bailey Circus train is home to the **entire** circus as it travels to over 90 cities all around the United States.

The 3.2-kilometer-long circus train is not your normal train with **coach** seats and a **snack** bar. Its train cars were specially designed for animals, people, and **equipment**.

The clowns, acrobats, dancers, and other performers sleep in rooms that are comfortable but small—about two meters long and two meters wide. The animals sleep in a separate part of the train, in their own specially designed cars.

The animal **caretakers** have their rooms near the animals, so they can make sure that the animals are always well cared for. If an elephant has a **sore** foot or if a tiger needs medicine, the animal trainers are right there to give them the care they need.

When the train **pulls into** a new city, all the animals and the equipment have to be **unloaded**. When the circus comes to New York, the elephants, horses, and other animals walk through the Lincoln Tunnel, a very busy tunnel 2.5 kilometers long, to get from the train to the circus. It takes six hours to unload the train. When the show is over, everything has to be **loaded** back on the train, and the circus **heads** for the next city and the next performances.

WHICH MEANING?
What does *bar* mean in line 9?

1 (*noun*) a pole or stick
2 (*verb*) forbid; not allow
3 (*noun*) a place to eat or drink

CHECK YOUR COMPREHENSION

Read the passage again and answer the questions. Circle your answers.

MAIN IDEA

1. What is this passage mainly about?

A. A small town
B. How a circus travels
C. Animals in the circus
D. How to care for animals

DETAIL

2. What can you find on the circus train?

A. Large rooms for performers
B. Coach seats and a snack bar
C. An animal training room
D. Special cars for animals

3. Where do the animal caretakers sleep?

A. In a room near the animals
B. In the front part of the train
C. In the same car as the clowns
D. In the same room as the tigers

4. What takes six hours?

A. Walking through Lincoln Tunnel
B. Traveling to the next city
C. Unloading the train
D. Loading the train

INFERENCE

5. Which statement is true about the Ringling Brothers and Barnum and Bailey Circus?

A. It isn't well-known.
B. It is a very big circus.
C. It doesn't have performing animals.
D. It travels to just a few areas of the country.

TEXT REFERENCE

6. In line 21, *so they can make sure*, what does the word *they* refer to?

A. Caretakers
B. Animals
C. Rooms
D. Cars

THINGS

PREPARE TO READ

Discuss these questions.

1. What is your favorite part of a circus performance?
2. Where do you think the first circus performances took place?

WORD FOCUS

Match the words with their definitions.

A.

1. attitude __	**a.** a ruler similar to a king
2. community __	**b.** a try
3. cultural __	**c.** feelings and thoughts about something
4. effort __	**d.** about a culture or society
5. emperor __	**e.** a group of people who live or work together

B.

1. festival __	**a.** an age group
2. generation __	**b.** a strong effect
3. impact __	**c.** a small town
4. look down upon __	**d.** a public party
5. village __	**e.** believe that someone is below you

SCAN

A. Guess the answer. Circle *a* or *b*.

Gold, Silver, and Bronze Lions are

a. circus animals. ***b.*** prizes for acrobats.

B. Scan the passage quickly to check your answer.

TRACK 10

The Chinese Circus

Over 2,000 years ago, during the Han Dynasty in China, common people searched for new ways to spend the long winter months. Because they had little work to do during this time of year, skilled workers, sailors, and farmers became acrobats, jugglers, and magicians. Their performances became part of the **village festivals**.

Entire families participated in these performances. Each **generation** taught its circus skills to the next generation. Children in these families began learning to perform while they were still babies. They were too young to understand the risks of their dangerous acrobatics, so they performed without fear. As young Chinese performers grew up, they taught their skills to others. The circus became a way of life for these families.

Though the ancient acrobats performed for **emperors**, **cultural attitudes** changed over time. Later on, acrobats were **looked down upon**. However, after 1949, the Chinese government made special **efforts** to bring the art form back to life. Since then, the Chinese circus has had a large **impact** on performing arts around the world.

The circus acrobats in today's China are all trained professionals, though they continue many of the ancient traditions. For example, they work with everyday items instead of special equipment. Each year, acrobats from all over China compete for the Gold, Silver, and Bronze Lions. These special prizes also represent a tradition. In many Asian cultures, people believe that the lion brings strength and health to the **community** and its people.

WHICH MEANING?

What does *long* mean in line 2?

1 (*adjective*) lasting a lot of time
2 (*verb*) want something very much
3 (*adjective*) continuing for a great distance

CHECK YOUR COMPREHENSION

Read the passage again and answer the questions. Circle your answers.

MAIN IDEA

1. What is this passage mainly about?
   - **A.** Chinese circus families
   - **B.** Ancient village festivals
   - **C.** Competitions for acrobats
   - **D.** History of the Chinese circus

DETAIL

2. Who were the original Chinese circus performers?
   - **A.** Lion trainers
   - **B.** Common people
   - **C.** Part of the government
   - **D.** Members of emperors' families

3. How did the ancient performers learn their circus skills?
   - **A.** From their families
   - **B.** At village schools
   - **C.** From the government
   - **D.** By watching people in their villages

4. What do lions represent in many Asian cultures?
   - **A.** Special prizes
   - **B.** Circus performers
   - **C.** Strength and health
   - **D.** The community and its people

INFERENCE

5. What did common people in ancient China probably do during the summer?
   - **A.** They juggled.
   - **B.** They worked.
   - **C.** They rested.
   - **D.** They traveled.

TEXT ORGANIZATION

6. Which paragraph talks about attitudes toward acrobats?
   - **A.** The first paragraph
   - **B.** The second paragraph
   - **C.** The third paragraph
   - **D.** The fourth paragraph

VOCABULARY REVIEW

MYSTERY PHRASE

Fill in the blanks. Then unscramble the letters in the circles to complete the mystery phrase.

1. Every [g e ◯ _ r _ t i _ n] in a circus family takes part in the act.
2. The town holds a [_ e _ ◯ i v _ l] every fall, and everyone has a fun time.
3. It takes a long time to [_ ◯ l o _ d] all of the circus animals off the truck.
4. The [◯ r _ g _ _ a _] Chinese circuses took place in the villages.
5. The performers made a special [◯ f f _ _ t] to tie in lessons for the children.
6. A [◯ _ m m u _ _ t _] is a group of people who live close together.
7. There are many [_ u l t _ ◯ a _] differences between the Chinese and American circuses.
8. That [p _ o _ e _ _ i _ _ ◯ l] acrobat gets paid to juggle.
9. One of the most important acrobatic skills is [p _ _ i e _ ◯ e].

Mystery phrase:

It takes a lot of [◯ ◯ ◯ ◯ ◯ ◯ ◯ ◯ ◯ t i o n] to juggle.

WORDS IN CONTEXT

Fill in the blanks with words from each box.

concentration	balanced	native	caretaker	juggled

1. I'm not a _______ of New York because I wasn't born there.
2. The clown _______ five balls at a time and never dropped one.
3. It takes a lot of _______ to study for a difficult test.
4. The acrobat _______ for a long time on one foot and didn't fall down.
5. The _______ has to feed the animals three times a day.

head	key	coach	equipment	long

6. If the weather is nice this weekend, we'll _______ for the beach.
7. You don't need much _______ for walking, just a good pair of shoes.
8. We had a pleasant train ride because the seats on the _______ were so comfortable.
9. I enjoy the _______ days of summer when the sun rises early.
10. Hard work is the _______ to reaching your goals.

perseverance	impact	village	entire	load

11. Before we leave on our trip, we'll have to _______ our suitcases into the car.
12. The job may be difficult, but with _______ you can do it.
13. Television has a big _______ on the attitudes of many people.
14. I grew up in a small _______, but I prefer living in the city.
15. We were so hungry that we ate the _______ cake.

WORD FAMILIES

Fill in the blanks with words from each box.

profession (*noun*)	**professional** (*adjective*)	**professionally** (*adverb*)

1. The _______ of an acrobat is difficult but interesting.
2. Only a _______ acrobat can do such a difficult trick.

patience (*noun*)	**patient** (*adjective*)	**patiently** (*adverb*)

3. Be _______! The bus will be here soon.
4. We waited for them _______, but they never arrived.

origin (*noun*)	**original** (*adjective*)	**originally** (*adverb*)

5. Nobody is sure of the exact _______ of the circus.
6. _______ he lived in San Francisco, but then he went to China.

WRONG WORD

One word in each group does not fit. Circle the word.

1.	emperor	king	father	prince
2.	snack	lunch	plate	breakfast
3.	thoughts	attitude	feelings	accomplishment
4.	city	car	village	town
5.	bar	restaurant	cafe	sandwich
6.	foot	sore	pain	hurt
7.	whole	part	entire	all

PHRASAL VERBS

Circle the correct words.

1. When we teach acrobatics, we can *tie* / *tie in* lessons about culture and history.
2. I learned to *tie* / *tie in* my shoes when I was very young.
3. I *looked* / *looked down upon* everywhere, but I couldn't find my glasses.
4. Not long ago, people *looked* / *looked down upon* actors and circus performers.
5. The horse *pulled* / *pulled into* the heavy wagon slowly up the hill.
6. By the time we *pulled* / *pulled into* the city, we were very tired.

WHAT ABOUT YOU?

Speaking

Ask your partner these questions.

1. What equipment do you need for your favorite sport?
2. What do you like to eat for a snack?
3. Which professions are you interested in?
4. Where will you head after school today?
5. What is an accomplishment you have made this year?

Writing

Now write about your partner. Use your partner's answers to the questions.

Example: Sue needs a ball and a racket for her favorite sport, tennis.

1. ____________________
2. ____________________
3. ____________________
4. ____________________
5. ____________________

READING QUIZ

Read the passage and answer the questions. Circle your answers.

Circus Program

Act 1: Unloading the Circus Train
In this original act, clowns pull a circus coach into the village (center stage) and unload all of the equipment for their festival (today's performance). They ask for help from the community (you, the audience).

Act 2: The Emperor's Dream
Traditionally, the Chinese circus was performed for the emperor. In this act, over twenty acrobats build a human castle. The emperor (played by Lu Quan) climbs to the top of the castle and falls asleep. The performance continues with the emperor's dream.

Act 3: Juggling
Professional jugglers Woo Chun, Lee Tao, and Hong Liang juggle everything from fans and bricks to great balls of fire. This begins as three separate acts and finishes as a team effort.

Act 4: Bamboo Balance
Lu Quan performs a fascinating balancing act. With amazing concentration, Quan walks, runs, and even skips rope on 1.8-meter-tall bamboo poles.

Act 5: A Tight Squeeze
In this final act, a young child (played by Shee Ping, who enrolled in the Chinese Circus School at age five) squeezes herself into many tiny objects. At last, the emperor wakes up feeling sore and uncomfortable!

BREAK (Time to grab a snack!)

MAIN IDEA

1. What is this passage mainly about?

A. A circus performance
B. A circus school
C. A circus clown
D. A circus train

DETAIL

2. Who builds a human castle?

A. The emperor
B. A young child
C. Twenty acrobats
D. Professional jugglers

INFERENCE

3. Where does the "festival" take place?

A. In a theater
B. In a train
C. In a castle
D. In a village

TEXT ORGANIZATION

4. In which act does the emperor wake up?

A. Act 2
B. Act 3
C. Act 4
D. Act 5

VOCABULARY

5. What does *unload* in line 4 mean?

A. Take off
B. Use
C. Pack
D. Look at

6. What does *snack* in line 34 mean?

A. Seat
B. Rest
C. Food
D. Ticket

UNIT 4

SHARKS

PEOPLE

PREPARE TO READ

Discuss these questions.

1. What do you know about sharks?
2. Eugenie Clark is fascinated by sharks. Why do you think so?

WORD FOCUS

Match the words with their definitions.

A.

1. aquarium __	a. a school like a university
2. college __	b. an animal
3. creature __	c. give completely
4. dedicate __	d. a tank where fish can live
5. degree __	e. a diploma from a university

B.

1. dive __	a. go under the water
2. inhabit __	b. happen
3. knowledge __	c. a type of fish
4. occur __	d. live in
5. shark __	e. a noun for *know*

SCAN

A. Guess if this is true or false. Circle *a* or *b*.

Eugenie Clark rode on the back of a shark.

a. True   ***b.*** False

B. Scan the passage quickly to check your answer.

TRACK 11

Eugenie Clark, the Shark Lady

One Saturday morning, a nine-year-old American girl and her Japanese mother visited an **aquarium** in New York City. The little girl was fascinated by all the fish swimming in the aquarium tanks. She visited the aquarium many times after that and learned everything she could about the ocean **creatures** that **inhabited** it.

That little girl was Eugenie Clark, and her first visit to the aquarium **occurred** over 75 years ago. She grew up to become the "**shark** lady," famous for her **knowledge** of sharks. Clark's knowledge came from her observations of sharks in the ocean where they lived naturally. She learned how to scuba **dive** so she didn't have to watch them in an aquarium tank. In the ocean she could swim right next to them or even ride them. Once, she rode a 12-meter whale shark.

Clark not only swam with fish, she also went to **college** to learn more about them. In 1940, it was unusual for a woman to get a doctorate **degree** in natural science. But, she had a great passion for her work, and she didn't let anything stop her.

Clark has **dedicated** her life to studying, writing, and teaching about fish, especially sharks. Even now in her eighties, she continues to dive to learn more about the 370 species of sharks. One of her favorite sharks is the lemon shark, which is a good student and can be trained. Humans are not the only ones to learn from Eugenie Clark.

WHICH MEANING?
What does *watch* mean in line 9?

1 (*noun*) guard
2 (*verb*) look at
3 (*noun*) small clock

CHECK YOUR COMPREHENSION

Read the passage again and answer the questions. Circle your answers.

MAIN IDEA

1. What is this passage mainly about?

A. Aquariums
B. A kind of fish
C. A shark expert
D. Diving

DETAIL

2. When did Eugenie Clark first visit an aquarium?

A. When she was nine years old
B. When she was a college student
C. When she was a mother
D. When she was 75 years old

3. How did Eugenie Clark learn about sharks?

A. She observed them in the ocean.
B. She studied them in college.
C. She swam next to them.
D. All of the above

4. How many species of sharks are there?

A. 12
B. Over 75
C. About 370
D. Nobody knows.

INFERENCE

5. According to this passage, what is true about the lemon shark?

A. It looks like a whale.
B. It is 12 meters long.
C. It learns well.
D. It is yellow.

TEXT REFERENCE

6. In line 4, *the ocean creatures that inhabited it*, what does the word *it* refer to?

A. The ocean
B. The aquarium
C. New York City
D. Japan

PLACES

a coral reef

PREPARE TO READ

Discuss these questions.

1. Have you ever tried scuba diving? If not, would you like to?
2. Where are the best places to go scuba diving?

WORD FOCUS

Match the words with their definitions.

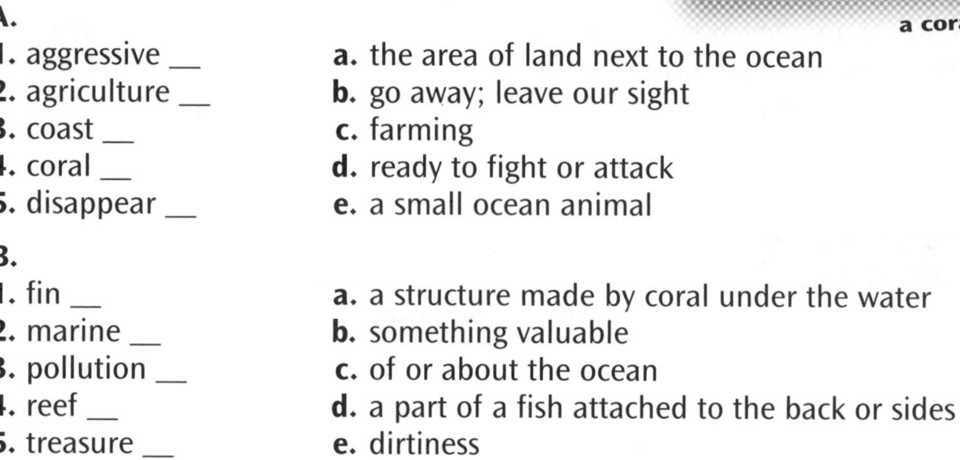

A.

1. aggressive __	**a.** the area of land next to the ocean
2. agriculture __	**b.** go away; leave our sight
3. coast __	**c.** farming
4. coral __	**d.** ready to fight or attack
5. disappear __	**e.** a small ocean animal

B.

1. fin __	**a.** a structure made by coral under the water
2. marine __	**b.** something valuable
3. pollution __	**c.** of or about the ocean
4. reef __	**d.** a part of a fish attached to the back or sides
5. treasure __	**e.** dirtiness

SCAN

A. Guess the answer. Circle *a* or *b*.

Where is the Great Barrier Reef?

a. Near Hawaii ***b.*** Near Australia

B. Scan the passage quickly to check your answer.

TRACK 12

The Great Barrier Reef

Along the eastern **coast** of Australia is one of the most fascinating areas of the natural world—the Great Barrier **Reef**. The Great Barrier Reef is more than 2,000 kilometers long, but it isn't really one long reef. It is actually made up of about 3,000 separate **coral** reefs.

The Great Barrier Reef is like a large city under the sea filled with many species of **marine** life. More than 2,000 species of fish inhabit it. There are also about 400 different species of coral and 500 species of seaweed. The fish include several kinds of sharks. The most common one is the blacktip reef shark. It gets its name from the black coloring on the <u>end</u> of its **fins**.

The blacktip shark isn't a dangerous shark, but there are dangerous animals on the reef. The tiger shark, for example, is an **aggressive** shark. There are several kinds of poisonous jellyfish, and there are poisonous sea snakes, too. Stingrays can injure people with their sharp tails. Divers have to be careful on the Great Barrier Reef.

Some animals on the reef are dangerous to people, but people are even more dangerous to the reef. **Agriculture** in Australia has caused water **pollution**, and this has already killed some areas of the reef. Divers cause damage when they take bits of coral from the reef, or when they stand on the reef. Unless humans learn to respect and protect natural **treasures** like the Great Barrier Reef, these treasures could one day **disappear** from the earth.

WHICH MEANING?
What does *end* mean in line 17?

1 (*noun*) edge or top
2 (*verb*) finish or stop
3 (*noun*) reason or purpose

CHECK YOUR COMPREHENSION

Read the passage again and answer the questions. Circle your answers.

MAIN IDEA

1. What is this passage mainly about?

A. Ocean pollution
B. Dangers on a reef
C. An interesting part of the world
D. Different kinds of marine animals

DETAIL

2. About how long is the Great Barrier Reef?

A. 500 kilometers
B. 2,000 kilometers
C. 3,000 kilometers
D. 4,000 kilometers

3. Which statement is true about the blacktip shark?

A. It is aggressive.
B. It has a sharp tail.
C. It is not very common.
D. It has black on its fins.

4. What causes water pollution?

A. Diving
B. Farming
C. Picking up coral
D. Standing on the reef

INFERENCE

5. Why do divers have to be careful on the Great Barrier Reef?

A. There are dangerous animals.
B. It's too far from the coast.
C. The water is very dirty.
D. It's difficult to stand on it.

TEXT ORGANIZATION

6. Which paragraph is about damage to the reef?

A. The first paragraph
B. The second paragraph
C. The third paragraph
D. The fourth paragraph

THINGS

a great white shark

PREPARE TO READ

Discuss these questions.

1. Are you afraid of sharks? Why or why not?
2. How large are great white sharks? What do they eat?

WORD FOCUS

Match the words with their definitions.

A.

1. birth __	**a.** find or meet
2. come across __	**b.** very big
3. dare __	**c.** the bone that holds your teeth
4. gigantic __	**d.** be brave enough
5. jaw __	**e.** a noun for *born*

B.

1. nutrition __	**a.** being alone
2. replace __	**b.** use something until it disappears
3. solitary __	**c.** take the place of
4. swallow __	**d.** move food from your mouth to your stomach
5. wear down __	**e.** food

SCAN

A. Guess if this is true or false. Circle *a* or *b*.

The great white shark has 300 teeth.

a. True   ***b.*** False

B. Scan the passage quickly to check your answer.

TRACK 13

Great White Sharks

Great white sharks are at the top of the ocean's food chain. They are the most aggressive sharks, and they have no natural predators. These giant marine creatures can grow up to six meters long and weigh as much as 1,800 kilos. Humans are the only beings who **dare** to get close to them.

Inside the **gigantic jaws** of a great white are thousands of teeth. Some teeth are for grabbing, while others are for tearing. A great white doesn't have to worry about losing its teeth. When they **wear down** or break, the shark grows extra teeth to **replace** them. Even with 3,000 teeth, it doesn't chew its food. Instead, it tears its prey into large pieces and **swallows** them whole.

Great white sharks are skillful hunters. All fish, even the smallest ones, produce small amounts of electricity. Great whites find their prey by feeling this electricity. It's impossible to hide from a great white shark.

Great whites are **solitary** creatures. This independence begins very early in life. Even before **birth**, the babies receive no **nutrition** from their mother. To survive, they eat their brothers and sisters. As soon as the surviving babies are born, the mother shark swims away and leaves the young sharks to begin life alone.

Although it normally lives a solitary life, the great white has **come across** humans too often. Because of the demand for shark teeth, jaws, and fins, the great white is now in danger of disappearing from the earth.

WHICH MEANING?
What does *break* mean in line 13?

1 (*noun*) a rest
2 (*verb*) divide into pieces
3 (*noun*) a chance; an opportunity

CHECK YOUR COMPREHENSION

Read the passage again and answer the questions. Circle your answers.

MAIN IDEA

1. What is this passage mainly about?

A. A large shark
B. Different predators
C. Shark mothers
D. The ocean's food chain

DETAIL

2. About how long are the longest great white sharks?

A. 3 meters
B. 6 meters
C. 16 meters
D. 18 meters

3. How does a great white shark eat?

A. Its mother feeds it.
B. It chews its food into small pieces.
C. It swallows large pieces of food.
D. It swallows only the smallest fish.

4. How does a great white shark find its prey?

A. It looks for bright colors.
B. It listens for sounds.
C. It feels electricity.
D. It smells very well.

INFERENCE

5. Why are great white sharks in danger of disappearing?

A. People kill them.
B. Their brothers and sisters eat them.
C. Their mothers don't feed them.
D. All of the above.

TEXT REFERENCE

6. In line 12, *When they wear down or break*, what does the word *they* refer to?

A. Teeth
B. Sharks
C. Prey animals
D. Pieces of food

VOCABULARY REVIEW

CROSSWORD PUZZLE

Complete the crossword using the clues.

Across

1. a creature with large jaws
2. opposite of tiny
6. an indoor place for fish
7. where the ocean meets the land

Down

1. being alone
3. live in
4. jump into water
5. You might come across this on an old ship at the bottom of the sea.
7. a place to study after high school

WORDS IN CONTEXT

Fill in the blanks with words from each box.

replace	watch	nutrition	reef	dare

1. Good _______ is important for our health.
2. I lost my house keys, so I had to _______ them.
3. It's fascinating to _______ fish in an aquarium.
4. I'm afraid of all sharks. I don't _______ to swim near them.
5. We visited a coral _______ and saw a lot of interesting fish.

dedicated	birth	ends	occurred	disappear

6. If we don't protect the coral reef, it could _______.
7. The _______ of the blacktip shark's fins are black.
8. My first trip to a reef _______ last summer.
9. After the _______ of her babies, the mother shark swims away.
10. The scientist _______ his life to protecting the great white shark.

agriculture	dive	break	came across	swallowed

11. Be careful! That box can _______ easily because it's made of glass.

12. The shark was very hungry and _______ its food quickly.

13. There's not much _______ in this area because the land isn't good for growing things.

14. While I was at the library, I _______ an interesting book about sharks.

15. I want to learn to _______ so I can watch fish under the water.

WORD FAMILIES

Fill in the blanks with words from each box.

aggressor (*noun*)	**aggressive** (*adjective*)	**aggressively** (*adverb*)

1. You need to be careful of sharks because some of them are very _______.

2. A great white shark is an _______ that attacks other fish.

pollution (*noun*)	**pollute** (*verb*)	**polluted** (*adjective*)

3. Cars and factories _______ the air.

4. The air in big cities is usually _______.

knowledge (*noun*)	**know** (*verb*)	**knowable** (*adjective*)

5. Eugenie Clark has a lot of _______ about sharks.

6. I don't _______ very much about marine life, but I'd like to learn more.

TRUE OR FALSE?

Are the following sentences true or false? Circle your answers.

1. Sharks have fins.	TRUE	FALSE
2. The coast is far from the ocean.	TRUE	FALSE
3. Marine creatures live on land.	TRUE	FALSE
4. You get a degree when you begin college.	TRUE	FALSE
5. Pollution makes the ocean clean.	TRUE	FALSE
6. Coral is an ocean animal.	TRUE	FALSE
7. Your teeth are in your jaw.	TRUE	FALSE

PHRASAL VERBS

Circle the correct words.

1. George and Maya always *come / come across* to school by bus.
2. We *came / came across* some friends at the mall yesterday.
3. I *wear / wear down* the bottoms of my shoes quickly because I walk a lot.
4. At many schools the students have to *wear / wear down* uniforms.
5. You can *come / come across* many different kinds of animals on a coral reef.
6. Always *wear / wear down* an extra sweater when the weather is cold.

WHAT ABOUT YOU?

Speaking

Ask your partner these questions.

1. What marine creatures are you interested in?
2. What is a treasure that you own?
3. What places on the coast would you like to visit?
4. What is the scariest animal you have come across?
5. What are some causes of pollution in your city?

Writing

Now write about your partner. Use your partner's answers to the questions.

Example: Sam is interested in whales, stingrays, and sea snakes.

1. ______________________________
2. ______________________________
3. ______________________________
4. ______________________________
5. ______________________________

READING QUIZ

Read the passage and answer the questions. Circle your answers.

The Great Shark Adventure

Where is the Great Shark Adventure?

The Great Shark Adventure takes place on Australia's Lizard Island. This island has over 24 beaches and is right on the Great Barrier Reef. Captain James Cook climbed to the peak of Lizard Island before he crossed the gigantic reef.

What training do I need?

We will give you all of the knowledge you need at our aquarium's Coral Reef College. First, you will learn about the marine life of the reef. Next, your class will separate into small groups for water training with our dedicated professional scuba divers. Finally, you will take a diving test. If you achieve 80% or more, you will get your "Diving Degree" and will be able to start on the Great Shark Adventure.

Is shark diving risky?

Many different sharks inhabit the Great Barrier Reef. Blacktip sharks are the species divers usually come across during the Great Shark Adventure. These sharks are not aggressive unless they fear a predator. Injuries to divers on the reef usually occur when creatures are eating or giving birth, or when divers foolishly dare to touch a shark's jaws or fins.

MAIN IDEA

1. What is the Great Shark Adventure?

- **A.** A book
- **B.** A movie
- **C.** A diving trip
- **D.** A college course

DETAIL

2. Where does the Great Shark Adventure take place?

- **A.** In Australia
- **B.** On Lizard Island
- **C.** On the Great Barrier Reef
- **D.** All of the above

INFERENCE

3. What is Coral Reef College?

- **A.** A university
- **B.** A travel agency
- **C.** A diving school
- **D.** A shark museum

TEXT REFERENCE

4. In line 14, *unless they fear a predator*, what does the word *they* refer to?

- **A.** Divers
- **B.** Sharks
- **C.** Injuries
- **D.** Species

VOCABULARY

5. What does *knowledge* in line 6 mean?

- **A.** Books
- **B.** Teachers
- **C.** Equipment
- **D.** Information

6. What does *aggressive* in line 14 mean?

- **A.** Dangerous
- **B.** Common
- **C.** Friendly
- **D.** Hungry

UNIT 5

SPORTS

Se Ri Pak

PEOPLE

PREPARE TO READ

Discuss these questions.

1. Do you like golf? How popular is it in your country?
2. Who are some famous golfers? Where are they from?

WORD FOCUS

Match the words with their definitions.

A.

1. attempt __	**a.** a place for dead people
2. career __	**b.** a sports trainer
3. cemetery __	**c.** make important
4. coach __	**d.** a profession
5. emphasize __	**e.** try

B.

1. overcome __	**a.** hard
2. qualify __	**b.** reaching a goal
3. rapid __	**c.** meet the requirements
4. success __	**d.** come out fine from a difficult situation
5. tough __	**e.** very fast

SCAN

A. Guess the answer. Circle *a* or *b*.

Who taught Se Ri Pak to play golf?

a. Her mother ***b.*** Her father

B. Scan the passage quickly to check your answer.

TRACK 14

Se Ri Pak

Early in her golf **career**, Korea's Se Ri Pak was given the nickname the Magic Princess. This nickname fits a young girl with such **rapid success**. Pak **qualified** for the LPGA (Ladies Professional Golf Association) just a few years after picking up her first golf club. While her success may seem magical, it was her hard work and dedication that made her famous.

As a young girl, Pak always carried her father's golf bag around the golf course. Since golf was a man's sport in Korea, she concentrated instead on training for track and field. When she was fourteen years old, her father finally decided to <u>hand</u> her a club to try. He soon could see that his daughter was a natural golfer and decided to be her **coach**.

Right from the beginning, her father **emphasized** the importance of mind control. To help her concentration, she used to look into a candle and think about her future career. Her father was a very **tough** coach. Some days he made her practice in freezing cold weather or before the sun rose. One time he required her to spend an entire night in a **cemetery** so that she would **overcome** her fears.

Pak later gave her father credit for her great success. In Florida, she qualified for the LPGA on her first **attempt**. In 2003, she competed in the Korean men's SBS Super Tournament, where she finished tenth. Within a few seasons after becoming a professional, Se Ri Pak became the most successful athlete in her country.

WHICH MEANING?
What does *hand* mean in line 8?

1 (*noun*) part of the body
2 (*verb*) give
3 (*noun*) helper

CHECK YOUR COMPREHENSION

Read the passage again and answer the questions. Circle your answers.

MAIN IDEA

1. What is this passage mainly about?

A. A professional golf competition
B. A famous princess
C. A successful golfer
D. A professional coach

DETAIL

2. Why did Pak originally train for track and field?

A. She wasn't interested in golf.
B. Her father was a track and field coach.
C. She was a natural runner.
D. Golf was a man's sport.

3. When did Pak begin to play golf?

A. When she was just a few years old
B. At the age of fourteen
C. After she went to Florida
D. In 2003

4. How did Pak practice concentration?

A. By training for track and field
B. By looking into a candle
C. By playing golf in cold weather
D. By sleeping in a cemetery

INFERENCE

5. Why is Pak called the Magic Princess?

A. Her rapid success seems like magic.
B. She likes to do magic tricks.
C. Her father is called the King of Golf.
D. She acts like a princess.

TEXT ORGANIZATION

6. Which paragraph mentions a Korean golf tournament?

A. The first paragraph
B. The second paragraph
C. The third paragraph
D. The fourth paragraph

PLACES

PREPARE TO READ

Discuss these questions.

1. What sports do people enjoy at the beach? How about you?
2. What sport is shown in the photo? Would you like to try it? Why or why not?

WORD FOCUS

Match the words with their definitions.

A.

1. boundaries __	**a.** put together
2. citizen __	**b.** collect
3. combine __	**c.** limits or edges
4. extreme __	**d.** a member of a nation
5. gather __	**e.** at a very high level

B.

1. huge __	**a.** begin a trip
2. set out __	**b.** pull
3. spread __	**c.** move in all directions
4. surface __	**d.** very big
5. tow __	**e.** top

SCAN

A. Guess if this is true or false. Circle *a* or *b*.

Kiteboarding is a very old sport.

a. True ***b.*** False

B. Scan the passage quickly to check your answer.

TRACK 15

Sea and Sky

Most sports take place in a stadium, in an arena, in a pool, or on a court. But some **extreme** sports have no **boundaries**. Kiteboarding is one extreme sport that uses both the open ocean and the air above as its playing field.

Imagine speeding over water at 25 kilometers an hour, jumping 15 meters into the air, and landing on the water again 100 meters away. This is the exciting sport of kiteboarding, a new sport that **combines** the skills of surfing and sailing. The sport's popularity has **spread** rapidly around the world. Now, it isn't unusual on a windy, sunny day at the beach to see large colorful kites high in the air as they **tow** kiteboarders along and above the water's **surface**. One extreme kiteboarding challenge took five kiteboarders from Florida, in the United States, to Cuba.

In 2002, Gilles d'Andreieux from France, an organizer of extreme sports events, **gathered** a team of professional kiteboarders to attempt to cross the sea from Key West, Florida to Vadero, Cuba. The team of five **set out** early in the morning and traveled all day, sometimes over waves as high as three meters or more. After kiteboarding for eight and a half hours, three of the five finally arrived on the Cuban coast. The three, **citizens** of Britain, France, and the United States, were worn out but happy. They had traveled 142 kilometers, through high waves and schools of flying fish. They had set the world record for the longest distance trip by kiteboard. That's a **huge** playing field.

WHICH MEANING?
What does *field* mean in line 3?

1 (*noun*) a place to play sports
2 (*verb*) respond to (a question)
3 (*noun*) a subject to study

CHECK YOUR COMPREHENSION

Read the passage again and answer the questions. Circle your answers.

MAIN IDEA

1. What is this passage mainly about?

A. An athlete from France
B. An exciting water sport
C. A trip across the sea
D. A day at the beach

DETAIL

2. Where do people practice kiteboarding?

A. At a swimming pool
B. On the sea
C. In a stadium
D. All of the above

3. What tows a kiteboarder?

A. A ship
B. A kite
C. A sailboat
D. A flying fish

4. In 2002, where did a team of five professional kiteboarders set out from?

A. France
B. Cuba
C. Britain
D. Florida

INFERENCE

5. What kind of person would probably enjoy kiteboarding?

A. A person who likes surfing and sailing
B. A person who prefers to be indoors
C. A person who likes safe sports
D. A person who travels to Cuba

TEXT REFERENCE

6. In line 15, *three of the five finally arrived*, what does the word *three* refer to?

A. Citizens of Britain
B. Organizers
C. Kiteboarders
D. Waves

THINGS

PREPARE TO READ

Discuss these questions.

1. What kinds of clothes do you wear for sports?
2. Why do people wear special sports uniforms?

WORD FOCUS

Match the words with their definitions.

A.

1. develop __	**a.** a level
2. innocence __	**b.** mean
3. rank __	**c.** grow and improve
4. represent __	**d.** inexperience
5. respect __	**e.** honor

B.

1. ripen __	**a.** be a sign of
2. root __	**b.** part of a plant that is underground
3. symbolize __	**c.** become ready over time; get near completion
4. treat __	**d.** understanding and knowledge
5. wisdom __	**e.** act in a certain way with people or things

SCAN

A. Guess the answer. Circle *a* or *b*.

In tae kwon do, a white belt represents

a. innocence. ***b.*** growth.

B. Scan the passage quickly to check your answer.

TRACK 16

Tae Kwon Do Belts and Uniforms

The tae kwon do uniform **symbolizes** the tradition of the sport, and the belt symbolizes the hard work and accomplishments of the student. The belt colors **represent** the growth of the students as they move through the **ranks** and **develop** their skills.

The belt color for the lowest rank is white. This color represents **innocence**. The student knows nothing about tae kwon do. The orange belt represents autumn, which is a season of changes. This shows that the student begins to <u>change</u> as she or he learns about tae kwon do. Yellow represents the earth. Just as a plant has **roots** in the earth, the student at this level is creating roots from which to grow. Green represents growth. The student's skills and knowledge are growing like a green plant. Blue represents the sky and means that the student continues to grow upward. Brown means that the student's skills are **ripening** like a fruit. Red represents danger. It is a warning to the student to use her or his skills and knowledge with **wisdom**. Black is the opposite of white. It is a combination of all the colors. It shows that the student has reached a high level of skill and knowledge.

The tae kwon do belt and uniform should always be **treated** with **respect**. This means that, in addition to keeping them neat and clean, students should only wear their belts and uniforms while practicing or performing the sport. Treating the belt and uniform with respect is an important part of the practice of tae kwon do.

WHICH MEANING?
What does *change* mean in line 7?

1 (*noun*) coins
2 (*verb*) replace
3 (*verb*) become different

CHECK YOUR COMPREHENSION

Read the passage again and answer the questions. Circle your answers.

MAIN IDEA

1. What is this passage mainly about?

A. The history of tae kwon do
B. The different levels of tae kwon do
C. The origin of the tae kwon do belt system
D. The meaning of tae kwon do belts and uniforms

DETAIL

2. What does a yellow belt symbolize?

A. Change
B. Roots
C. Growth
D. Sky

3. Which color belt gives the student a warning?

A. White
B. Blue
C. Brown
D. Red

4. Which color belt represents the highest rank?

A. Black
B. Brown
C. Green
D. Orange

INFERENCE

5. How do students show respect for their uniforms?

A. By wearing them all the time
B. By earning as many belts as possible
C. By taking good care of them
D. By practicing the sport often

TEXT REFERENCE

6. In line 3, *as they move through the ranks*, what does the word *they* refer to?

A. Belts
B. Accomplishments
C. Students
D. Levels

VOCABULARY REVIEW

CROSSWORD PUZZLE

Complete the crossword using the clues.

Across

2. difficult
6. understanding and knowledge
7. a level
8. a childlike characteristic
10. try

Down

1. limits you can't go beyond
3. very quick
4. put more than one thing together
5. stand for something else (as a symbol)
9. a place to bury the dead

WORDS IN CONTEXT

Fill in the blanks with words from each box.

citizen	field	boundary	coach	surface

1. I had a very good _______ who taught me how to play tennis.
2. That fence marks the _______ of our land.
3. I'm not a _______ of this country even though I live here.
4. There is a big _______ behind our school where we play soccer.
5. The _______ of the road was not very smooth.

qualify	ripen	represents	gather	spread

6. High school students usually _______ at the mall on Saturday afternoon.
7. Tae kwon do is from Korea, but interest in the sport has _______ all around the world.
8. Let those green apples _______ before you pick them.
9. Only very good golfers _______ for top competitions.
10. Our flag _______ our country.

overcame	rank	developed	emphasized	set out

11. My parents have always _______ the importance of a good education.

12. I was afraid of the test, but I _______ my fears and got a good grade.

13. We _______ on our trip early in the morning because we had a long way to go.

14. I _______ good golf skills by practicing every day.

15. I just started to learn tae kwon do, so I'm still at the lowest _______.

WORD FAMILIES

Fill in the blanks with words from each box.

symbol (*noun*)	**symbolize** (*verb*)	**symbolic** (*adjective*)

1. Blue tae kwon do belts _______ the sky.

2. The tae kwon do uniform is _______ of a tradition.

success (*noun*)	**succeed** (*verb*)	**successful** (*adjective*)

3. Se Ri Pak's parents are very proud of her _______.

4. If you want to be _______ in sports, you have to practice a lot.

wisdom (*noun*)	**wise** (*adjective*)	**wisely** (*adverb*)

5. My grandmother is a very _______ person.

6. She answers all my questions _______.

SYNONYMS OR ANTONYMS?

Look at the word pairs. Are the words synonyms, antonyms, or neither? Check the correct answer.

		Synonyms	Antonyms	Neither
1. career	profession	☐	☐	☐
2. set out	arrive	☐	☐	☐
3. tow	push	☐	☐	☐
4. hand	give	☐	☐	☐
5. wisdom	innocence	☐	☐	☐
6. root	tree	☐	☐	☐
7. huge	gigantic	☐	☐	☐
8. treat	respect	☐	☐	☐

SENTENCE COMPLETION

Complete the postcard with words from the box.

develop	rapidly	extreme	changed	surface

Hey Cindy,

You'll never guess what I did at the beach today! I learned a new ______ sport–kiteboarding. It's exciting because you can move so ______. It's like flying. Today the ______ of the water was calm with few waves, so I had an easy time. I'm going to take another lesson tomorrow because I want to continue to ______ my skills. I used to prefer indoor sports, but now I've ______.

Kiteboarding is the only sport for me! Maybe you can learn it, too.

See you soon.

Richard

WHAT ABOUT YOU?

Speaking

Ask your partner these questions.

1. Where do you often gather with your friends?
2. Which extreme sports would you like to try?
3. What is something tough that you have done?
4. How rapidly can you run?
5. Who is a wise person that you know?

Writing

Now write about your partner. Use your partner's answers to the questions.

Example: Rita often gathers with her friends in the school cafeteria.

1. ______________________________
2. ______________________________
3. ______________________________
4. ______________________________
5. ______________________________

READING QUIZ

Read the passage and answer the questions. Circle your answers.

To: kimshin@worldpenpals.com
From: parkjinho@worldpenpals.com
Subject: kiteboarding

Hi Shin,

It's fun writing e-mails in English, isn't it? Today I am going to tell you about my favorite sport. I have been kiteboarding for three years. The popularity of this sport has spread rapidly at my school. My friends and I gather at the beach every Saturday to surf or kiteboard. My dream is to qualify for the Korean teen kiteboarding team next summer. (I set out to qualify this year, but I injured my leg.) Do you like sports? Write soon!

To: parkjinho@worldpenpals.com
From: kimshin@worldpenpals.com
Subject: Re: kiteboarding

Hi Jin-ho,

Thanks for your e-mail. Yes, I love sports! It's fascinating that you are a kiteboarder. I have a friend who kiteboards. He ranks 10th in China for teens, and he wants to make kiteboarding his career. I like to watch extreme sports, but I haven't attempted to play any. First I have to overcome my fear of water! Right now my favorite sport is golf. It combines mental and physical skills. My brother is a professional golfer, so he is a very tough coach. He always emphasizes that concentration is at the root of the game. Write again soon!

MAIN IDEA

1. What are these e-mail messages about?

A. Extreme sports
B. Kiteboarding teams
C. Favorite sports
D. Golf games

DETAIL

2. Who likes to kiteboard?

A. Jin-ho
B. Shin's friend
C. Jin-ho's friends
D. All of the above

3. What does Jin-ho want to do next summer?

A. Visit Shin
B. Learn to play golf
C. Become part of a team
D. Go surfing everyday

INFERENCE

4. Who is teaching Shin to play golf?

A. Jin-ho
B. Shin's friend
C. Shin's brother
D. Jin-ho's friend

VOCABULARY

5. What does *rapidly* in line 4 mean?

A. Slowly
B. Unusually
C. Quickly
D. Often

6. What does *tough* in line 13 mean?

A. Hard
B. Fun
C. Good
D. Nice

UNIT 6

MONSTERS

PEOPLE

Count Dracula

PREPARE TO READ

Discuss these questions.

1. What are some monster movies that you've seen?
2. What do you know about Count Dracula?

WORD FOCUS

Match the words with their definitions.

A.

1. coffin __	**a.** very bad
2. devil __	**b.** a box for burying a dead person
3. dragon __	**c.** a large, scary animal in stories
4. evil __	**d.** a very bad spirit or creature
5. identify __	**e.** say or know the name of someone or something

B.

1. myth __	**a.** believing in things not based on fact
2. reflection __	**b.** a common story or belief
3. superstitious __	**c.** what you see in a mirror
4. vampire __	**d.** an injured person
5. victim __	**e.** a person in stories who drinks blood; Dracula

SCAN

A. Guess if this is true or false. Circle *a* or *b*.

Dracula doesn't have a shadow.

a. True ***b.*** False

B. Scan the passage quickly to check your answer.

TRACK 17

Count Dracula

While the <u>rest</u> of the world sleeps, one man is awake. He lives in a cold, solitary castle in the mountains of eastern Europe. During the day, he sleeps in a **coffin** filled with dirt. At night, he wakes up hungry. . .for blood! He's Count Dracula, the **vampire** from Transylvania.

The character of Count Dracula comes from the novel, *Dracula*, written by Bram Stoker in 1897. Since then, the character in Stoker's novel has appeared in many movies and stories, in which Dracula travels around at night looking for **victims**. When he comes across one, he sucks blood from the victim's neck. People can protect themselves from Dracula by hanging garlic around the doors and windows of their houses. They can **identify** him by looking for his **reflection** in a mirror. He doesn't have one, and he doesn't have a shadow, either.

Many people think that Stoker got the idea for his Dracula from a man named Vlad Tepes who lived in Transylvania 600 years ago. Tepes sometimes used the name Dracula, which comes from a word that means **dragon** or **devil**. This is probably the only connection between the character Dracula and the real man in history.

Stoker invented his character and story, but some of his ideas came from traditional stories. Around the world there are still **myths** about vampires. **Superstitious** people believe that the dead can return to the world and suck the blood of living people. Believers close their windows at night to keep out the **evil** night air—and Dracula.

WHICH MEANING?
What does *rest* mean in line 1?

1 (*noun*) all the others
2 (*verb*) relax
3 (*noun*) a musical term

CHECK YOUR COMPREHENSION

Read the passage again and answer the questions. Circle your answers.

MAIN IDEA

1. What is this passage mainly about?

A. A novel
B. An author
C. A story character
D. A superstitious person

DETAIL

2. People use ________ to protect themselves from Dracula.

A. garlic
B. novels
C. dragons
D. coffins

3. Dracula likes the taste of

A. garlic.
B. dirt.
C. blood.
D. All of the above

4. What does the name Dracula mean?

A. Vampire
B. Bloody
C. Victim
D. Devil

INFERENCE

5. Who was Vlad Tepes?

A. A real man
B. A vampire
C. A story character
D. A friend of Dracula

TEXT REFERENCE

6. In line 10, *He doesn't have one*, what does the word *one* refer to?

A. A mirror
B. A reflection
C. A shadow
D. A house

PLACES

PREPARE TO READ

Discuss these questions.

1. What do you know about the Loch Ness monster?
2. What other mysterious creatures have you heard about?

WORD FOCUS

Match the words with their definitions.

A.

1. century __	a. be
2. chilly __	b. cold
3. claim __	c. supporting facts
4. evidence __	d. a period of 100 years
5. exist __	e. say that something is true

B.

1. hoax __	a. a traditional story
2. investigate __	b. a trick or lie
3. legend __	c. result
4. resemble __	d. look for information
5. turn out __	e. look like

SCAN

A. Guess if this is true or false. Circle *a* or *b*.

Many people have seen a monster in Loch Ness.

a. True ***b.*** False

B. Scan the passage quickly to check your answer.

TRACK 18

Loch Ness and Its Monster

In northern Scotland there is a long, deep lake called Loch Ness. More than 200 meters deep, it is the largest lake in the United Kingdom. Hiding in its dark, **chilly** waters lives a gigantic monster. It weighs more than 1,000 kilos and is at least ten meters long. Its color is dark gray. Some people say it has a head like a horse. Others say it **resembles** a snake. Many people travel to Loch Ness to look for this strange monster, but only a few people have seen it. At least, they **claim** they have seen it.

The Loch Ness Monster is a famous **legend**. The first story about a monster in Loch Ness was told over 500 years ago, but the legend of the monster became popular only in the twentieth **century**. In 1933, a husband and wife reported that they saw a gigantic monster in the middle of the lake. Since then, a number of people have claimed that they have seen a monster in Loch Ness. Several people have taken photographs, but at least one of them **turned out** to be a **hoax**. During the 1960s, an organization was formed to **investigate** the monster. They took many photographs and made movies, but they were never able to identify a monster.

There is no real **evidence** that a monster **exists** in Loch Ness, but there is also no evidence that one doesn't exist. One thing is true about Loch Ness: there are a lot of superstitious tourists there.

WHICH MEANING?
What does *story* mean in line 16?

1 (*noun*) the floor of a house or building
2 (*noun*) a lie
3 (*noun*) a tale, legend, or myth

CHECK YOUR COMPREHENSION

Read the passage again and answer the questions. Circle your answers.

MAIN IDEA

1. What is this passage mainly about?

A. A legend about a monster
B. Tourism at Loch Ness
C. A couple that saw a monster
D. Animal life in Loch Ness

DETAIL

2. What do people say about the Loch Ness monster?

A. It weighs about 100 kilos.
B. Its color is light gray.
C. It makes a sound like a horse.
D. It looks like a snake.

3. When did people first talk about the Loch Ness monster?

A. 500 years ago
B. 200 years ago
C. In 1933
D. In 1960

4. In the 1960s, what did an organization do?

A. It saw a big monster in the middle of the lake.
B. It tried to find the monster.
C. It told a hoax about the monster.
D. It showed the monster to tourists.

INFERENCE

5. Who has proven that there is a monster in Loch Ness?

A. A special organization
B. Several tourists
C. A husband and wife
D. No one

TEXT REFERENCE

6. In line 27, *at least one of them*, what does the word *one* refer to?

A. A photograph
B. A person
C. A monster
D. A movie

THINGS

PREPARE TO READ

Discuss these questions.

1. What stories do you know about dragons? What are some of their characteristics?
2. Do you think dragons are good or evil?

WORD FOCUS

Match the words with their definitions.

A.

1. advice __	**a.** normal
2. associate __	**b.** terrible
3. average __	**c.** attractive characteristic
4. charm __	**d.** connect
5. dreadful __	**e.** help; suggestions

B.

1. god __	**a.** a class of animals with cold blood and rough skin
2. powerful __	**b.** stop
3. prevent __	**c.** an injury
4. reptile __	**d.** a spirit
5. wound __	**e.** strong; able to do many things

SCAN

A. Guess the answer. Circle *a* or *b*.

People once believed that a dragon's _______ could protect them.

a. skin ***b.*** blood

B. Scan the passage quickly to check your answer.

TRACK 19

Dragons

This gigantic animal has the skin of a **reptile**, the body of an elephant, the head of a horse, and the tail of a lizard. Among its many other **charms**, it breathes fire. It's not your **average** household pet, but perhaps it should be. Some cultures think a dragon is a wise creature that brings good luck. Others think it is a **dreadful** monster that destroys things.

Dragons are important in the myths of many Asian countries. They are wise and **powerful** creatures. They are **associated** with the **gods** and the emperors. They can give **advice**, and they represent good luck. However, they can also become angry when people don't respect them. Then, they can become destructive. Dragons might cause big storms or damage people's houses. It is important to treat dragons well to **prevent** their anger.

In myths of western countries, dragons are powerful, magical creatures, but they aren't usually good. In many stories they are evil creatures, and people fear them. They are large animals that resemble scary snakes with legs. They breathe fire. People don't try to treat dragons well; they try to kill them.

In some stories dragons are good and wise. In others they are evil monsters. Whether a dragon is good or evil, it is always a symbol of strength and magic. Long ago, some superstitious people believed myths that dragons' blood could protect them from **wounds**. Some also believed that if they drank dragons' blood, they would be able to understand the speech of animals. In the myths of Asia and the West, dragons are powerful and magical creatures.

WHICH MEANING?
What does *fire* mean in line 2?

1 (*verb*) shoot a gun
2 (*noun*) something that burns
3 (*verb*) take away someone's job

CHECK YOUR COMPREHENSION

Read the passage again and answer the questions. Circle your answers.

MAIN IDEA

1. What is this passage mainly about?
- **A.** A creature in myths
- **B.** An Asian legend
- **C.** Methods of magic
- **D.** Types of reptiles

DETAIL

2. In Asia, what do dragons represent?
- **A.** Evil
- **B.** Luck
- **C.** Fear
- **D.** Pets

3. In western myths, how do people treat dragons?
- **A.** They give advice to dragons.
- **B.** They burn dragons with fire.
- **C.** They try to kill dragons.
- **D.** They damage dragons' houses.

4. What do people believe about dragons?
- **A.** They are magical.
- **B.** They are strong.
- **C.** They are evil.
- **D.** All of the above

INFERENCE

5. What do some myths say about dragons' blood?
- **A.** It is magical.
- **B.** It is poisonous.
- **C.** It is destructive.
- **D.** It is delicious.

TEXT ORGANIZATION

6. Which paragraph is about dragon myths in the West?
- **A.** The first paragraph
- **B.** The second paragraph
- **C.** The third paragraph
- **D.** The fourth paragraph

VOCABULARY REVIEW

WORD SEARCH

Look for the following words in the square. Then look for the hidden message formed by unused letters in the first two lines of the puzzle.

- advice
- associate
- coffin
- dreadful
- evidence
- exist
- identify
- legend
- superstitious
- victim
- wound

V	A	M	N	P	I	R	E	S	D	R	I	N	K	E
B	L	O	I	O	D	H	L	Y	S	F	O	S	C	L
R	G	V	F	N	V	P	J	U	H	Q	U	N	J	A
C	K	U	F	X	G	V	A	Q	F	O	E	A	Q	D
A	S	S	O	C	I	A	T	E	I	D	D	U	N	Z
M	I	T	C	I	V	S	W	T	I	V	A	U	B	L
V	L	D	U	J	A	G	I	V	I	S	O	E	T	L
K	B	I	E	T	Z	T	E	C	H	W	K	U	R	O
R	T	E	S	N	S	G	E	L	H	L	C	D	U	D
M	C	I	T	R	T	D	F	U	N	S	F	D	U	L
T	X	K	E	F	O	I	D	N	E	G	E	L	H	G
E	N	P	J	A	X	N	F	Q	R	T	S	F	V	A
Y	U	W	B	V	H	Q	N	Y	N	J	Z	T	C	U
S	O	Z	A	S	B	B	F	X	J	M	H	B	Y	U

Hidden message:

☐☐☐☐☐☐☐☐ ☐☐☐☐☐ ☐☐☐☐☐.

WORDS IN CONTEXT

Fill in the blanks with words from each box.

turn out	reflection	prevent	rest	claim

1. Sally took just one sandwich and left the _______ on the plate.
2. I couldn't see my _______ well because the mirror was so dirty.
3. Bob and Sue _______ that they met a movie star, but I don't believe it.
4. If you study hard, your test will _______ well.
5. You can _______ accidents by driving carefully.

advice	devils	exist	chilly	average

6. Those children always shout and fight and act like little _______.
7. Today was an _______ day for me—nothing special happened.
8. Dress warmly because it's _______ today.
9. Dragons aren't real; they only _______ in stories.
10. I don't know what to do. Can you give me some _______?

resembles	hoax	gods	dreadful	superstitious

11. In many myths, people ask the _______ for help.
12. Only _______ people are afraid of vampires.
13. The photograph wasn't real; it was just a _______.
14. Sarah _______ her mother but looks nothing like her father.
15. There was a _______ storm last night that caused a lot of damage.

WORD FAMILIES

Fill in the blanks with words from each box.

investigations (*noun*)	**investigator** (*noun*)	**investigate** (*verb*)

1. People have made many _______, but they still can't find evidence of a monster.
2. People still go to Loch Ness because they want to _______ the legend.

power (*noun*)	**powerful** (*adjective*)	**powerfully** (*adverb*)

3. Dragons are strong creatures that have a lot of _______.
4. The wind blew _______ all night.

charm (*noun*)	**charms** (*verb*)	**charming** (*adjective*)

5. Many people are attracted to Jane because she is such a _______ person.
6. She always _______ people with her funny stories.

TRUE OR FALSE?

Are the following sentences true or false? Circle your answers.

1. A myth is a true story.	TRUE	FALSE
2. A lizard is a type of reptile.	TRUE	FALSE
3. Fire is cold.	TRUE	FALSE
4. A century lasts 100 years.	TRUE	FALSE
5. Vampires really exist.	TRUE	FALSE

SYNONYMS OR ANTONYMS?

Look at the word pairs. Are the words synonyms, antonyms, or neither? Check the correct answer.

		Synonyms	Antonyms	Neither
1. chilly	warm	☐	☐	☐
2. dragon	vampire	☐	☐	☐
3. hoax	lie	☐	☐	☐
4. wound	injury	☐	☐	☐
5. century	year	☐	☐	☐
6. evil	good	☐	☐	☐

WHAT ABOUT YOU?

Speaking

Ask your partner these questions.

1. Who usually gives you advice?

2. Who do you resemble?

3. What kinds of stories do you like?

4. What do you do when the weather is chilly?

5. What would you do if you met a vampire?

Writing

Now write about your partner. Use your partner's answers to the questions.

Example: Tim's older brother usually gives him advice.

1. ______________________________

2. ______________________________

3. ______________________________

4. ______________________________

5. ______________________________

READING QUIZ

Read the passage and answer the questions. Circle your answers.

Teenzine—Issue 10

October is Monster Mystery Month.

Have a costume party!

First, make a list of monsters you want at your party. Next, ask your friends to come to the party dressed as Dracula, Frankenstein, and other evil creatures. Finally, make your house resemble a monster's home.

Advice on how to make your average monster feel at home:

- Build a coffin. Cut the top off a long box and paint it black. Put it at the front door.
- Put a victim in your coffin. You can dress up a real person or use a doll. Give your victim wounds, such as vampire bites.
- Turn off most of the lights in your house. People associate darkness with evil.
- Leave the windows open to make the house feel chilly!
- Draw on mirrors. When people look at their reflection they might see a devil, too.
- Turn the monsters (your guests) into investigators. The first monster to find and identify the secret dragon wins. You can give the winner a book on myths or superstitions.
- Prevent people from entering bedrooms or other areas by putting dreadful pictures on the doors. Add *DO NOT ENTER* signs.

****Write and tell us how your party turned out!***

MAIN IDEA

1. What is the main purpose of this passage?

A. To describe Dracula's house
B. To present ideas for planning a party
C. To give instructions for making costumes
D. To explain how to protect yourself from monsters

DETAIL

2. How can you prepare your house for a monster party?

A. Hang signs on doors
B. Open windows
C. Turn off the lights
D. All of the above

3. What should you put at the front door?

A. A coffin
B. A vampire
C. A mirror
D. A light

INFERENCE

4. What would NOT be a good costume to wear at this party?

A. A doll
B. A devil
C. A dragon
D. A vampire

VOCABULARY

5. What does *chilly* in line 22 mean?

A. Scary
B. Dangerous
C. Cold
D. Strange

6. What does *evil* in line 6 mean?

A. Funny
B. Unusual
C. Interesting
D. Bad

UNIT 7

MUSIC

Han-na Chang

PEOPLE

PREPARE TO READ

Discuss these questions.

1. Do you like classical music? What other kinds of music do you like?
2. Who are your favorite musicians? What do you like about them and their music?

WORD FOCUS

Match the words with their definitions.

A.

1. arrange __	a. a musical instrument like a large violin
2. astounded __	b. the leader of a group of musicians
3. cello __	c. organize
4. conductor __	d. very big
5. enormous __	e. very surprised

B.

1. interfere __	a. get in the way; prevent
2. orchestra __	b. meaningful; important
3. philosophy __	c. a group of musicians
4. significant __	d. special ability
5. talent __	e. the study of ideas and beliefs

SCAN

A. Guess the answer. Circle *a* or *b*.

Where was Han-na Chang born?

a. Korea *b.* New York

B. Scan the passage quickly to check your answer.

TRACK 20

Han-na Chang

Han-na Chang became famous when she was still a child in middle school. A native of Korea, she started playing the piano at the age of three. At the age of six, she began playing the **cello**, and she hasn't put it down since. When Chang was ten, she and her family moved to New York. There, she went to school, learned English, and kept on playing the cello.

Chang entered the International Cello Competition in Paris in 1994. She was just eleven years old. Since she wasn't much bigger than her cello, everyone was **astounded** by her huge **talent**. After she won the competition, she began playing concerts in different places around the world. She played her first concert in Seoul in 1995 and her first concert at Carnegie Hall in New York in 1996. She has played with some of the most famous **orchestras** and **conductors** in the world. She has also recorded several CDs and won several more prizes.

Chang tried not to let her busy concert schedule **interfere** with her education. She **arranged** her concerts so that she could still attend school, make friends, and have a normal life. When she graduated from high school, she went to Harvard University and studied **philosophy**, not music. Chang loves playing music, and she also enjoys having friends and activities that aren't associated with music. But music, of course, is extremely **significant** in her life. She continues to tour and record, sharing her **enormous** talent with audiences around the world.

WHICH MEANING?
What does *moved* mean in line 4?

1 (*verb*) went forward
2 (*verb*) went to live in a new place
3 (*verb*) caused deep feelings

CHECK YOUR COMPREHENSION

Read the passage again and answer the questions. Circle your answers.

MAIN IDEA

1. What is this passage mainly about?

A. Cello concerts
B. A cello school
C. Cello competitions
D. A young cello player

DETAIL

2. When did Chang first play the cello?

A. At the age of three
B. At the age of six
C. At the age of ten
D. At the age of eleven

3. What did Chang do in 1994?

A. She entered an international competition.
B. She played a concert at Carnegie Hall.
C. She entered Harvard University.
D. She played a concert in Seoul.

4. What did Chang study at Harvard University?

A. Philosophy
B. Education
C. English
D. Music

INFERENCE

5. Why did Chang surprise people in Paris?

A. She had already won several prizes.
B. She could speak excellent English.
C. She had an enormous cello.
D. She was very young.

TEXT REFERENCE

6. In line 3, *and she hasn't put it down since*, what does the word *it* refer to?

A. Music
B. The piano
C. The cello
D. School

PLACES

Carnegie Hall

PREPARE TO READ

Discuss these questions.

1. What are some famous concert halls that you know about?
2. Why do you think musicians like to play at Carnegie Hall?

WORD FOCUS

Match the words with their definitions.

A.

1. acoustics __	**a.** a funny story
2. case __	**b.** a person who writes music
3. composer __	**c.** the quality of sound
4. highlight __	**d.** a box for holding something
5. joke __	**e.** the best part or moment

A.

1. privilege __	**a.** famous; important
2. prominent __	**b.** really
3. superb __	**c.** an honor
4. truly __	**d.** excellent
5. wander __	**e.** walk around

SCAN

A. Guess the answer. Circle *a* or *b*.

Andrew Carnegie was a famous

a. musician. ***b.*** rich man.

B. Scan the passage quickly to check your answer.

TRACK 21

CARNEGIE HALL

A concert violinist went to New York City to play at Carnegie Hall. It was his first visit to the city, and he got lost on the way from his hotel to the concert. After **wandering** up and down several streets, he decided to ask for directions. "Excuse me," he said to a woman on the corner. "How do I get to Carnegie Hall?" The woman looked at the man holding his violin **case** and answered, "Practice, practice, practice."

In this old **joke**, *get to Carnegie Hall* has two meanings: (1) arrive at the building called Carnegie Hall; (2) reach the top of the music profession, symbolized by Carnegie Hall. To perform at Carnegie Hall is a **privilege** for any musician. It is the **highlight** of his or her career. It **truly** takes a lot of practice and hard work to be good enough to play at Carnegie Hall.

Carnegie Hall was built by Andrew Carnegie, one of the richest men of his time. It opened in May of 1891. It is famous for its **superb acoustics**, which make it a wonderful place to both perform and listen to music—all types of music. The famous Russian **composer** Tchaikovsky played there, and so did the Beatles.

Since opening night over 100 years ago, many **prominent** classical, jazz, and pop musicians have performed at Carnegie Hall. Whether they arrived on the night of their performances by subway, taxi, or on foot, they all got there by dedication to their art, talent—and practice, practice, practice.

WHICH MEANING?
What does *takes* mean in line 10?

1 (*verb*) steals
2 (*verb*) carries
3 (*verb*) requires

CHECK YOUR COMPREHENSION

Read the passage again and answer the questions. Circle your answers.

MAIN IDEA

1. What is this passage mainly about?
   - **A.** A rich man
   - **B.** Types of music
   - **C.** Famous musicians
   - **D.** A place to play music

DETAIL

2. What did the violinist in the joke want to know?
   - **A.** The way to the concert hall
   - **B.** The Carnegie Hall concert schedule
   - **C.** Where to buy concert tickets
   - **D.** How to play the violin well

3. When was Carnegie Hall built?
   - **A.** In 1891
   - **B.** Almost 100 years ago
   - **C.** About 18 years ago
   - **D.** In 1981

4. What do Tchaikovsky and the Beatles have in common?
   - **A.** They were friends of Andrew Carnegie.
   - **B.** They were classical musicians.
   - **C.** They performed at Carnegie Hall.
   - **D.** They got lost on the way to a concert.

INFERENCE

5. Most musicians who perform at Carnegie Hall
   - **A.** play classical music.
   - **B.** arrive by subway.
   - **C.** feel privileged.
   - **D.** are rich people.

TEXT ORGANIZATION

6. Which paragraph explains the meaning of the joke about Carnegie Hall?
   - **A.** The first paragraph
   - **B.** The second paragraph
   - **C.** The third paragraph
   - **D.** The fourth paragraph

THINGS

a cello

PREPARE TO READ

Discuss these questions.

1. What musical instruments do you like? Which ones can you play?
2. How much do you think a good cello costs? What about other musical instruments?

WORD FOCUS

Match the words with their definitions.

A.

1. cabinet __	**a.** make
2. craft __	**b.** one by one
3. economical __	**c.** a type of furniture
4. individually __	**d.** inexpensive
5. investment __	**e.** a way to make your money grow

B.

1. lead __	**a.** notice
2. mass-produced __	**b.** value
3. spy __	**c.** taken from the owner
4. stolen __	**d.** the most important
5. worth __	**e.** made in large quantities

SCAN

A. Guess the answer. Circle *a* or *b*.

When was Han-na Chang's cello made?

a. In 1757 ***b.*** In 1997

B. Scan the passage quickly to check your answer.

TRACK 22

A Stolen Cello

One day, Melanie Stevens was on the way to work in Los Angeles. She **spied** a cello beside a trash can. Melanie decided to take it home so her boyfriend, a furniture maker, could turn it into a **cabinet** to <u>hold</u> CDs.

A few days later, Melanie saw a TV news report about a **stolen** cello. It had been stolen from the home of the **lead** cellist of the Los Angeles Philharmonic Orchestra. It was **worth** 3.5 million dollars. "That's a lot of money for a CD cabinet!" thought Melanie. She returned the cello immediately.

Why was the stolen cello worth so much money? It was made in 1684 by Antonio Stradivari, one of the great instrument makers of history. It was one of only 60 cellos that he ever made. Other prominent cello makers include Andrea Amati and Giovanni Guadagnini. They carefully **crafted** their musical instruments by hand so that their cellos would make the most beautiful sounds possible.

In the nineteenth century, people began to make **mass-produced** cellos instead of crafting them **individually** by hand. These cellos were more **economical** to make, but they didn't sound as beautiful as the old cellos. In the middle of the twentieth century, wealthy people began to buy the old hand-crafted instruments as **investments**. Back then, they were worth $2,500 to $40,000. Today they are worth millions.

Great musicians want to play great instruments. Han-na Chang, for example, plays a Guadagnini that was made in 1757. To make beautiful music you need a beautiful instrument.

WHICH MEANING?
What does *hold* mean in line 3?

1 (*noun*) power over something or someone
2 (*verb*) keep or store
3 (*verb*) run (a meeting)

CHECK YOUR COMPREHENSION

Read the passage again and answer the questions. Circle your answers.

MAIN IDEA

1. What is this passage mainly about?

A. Valuable cellos
B. Cello makers
C. Cello players
D. Stolen cellos

DETAIL

2. What did Melanie Stevens do with the cello that she found?

A. She learned how to play it.
B. She gave it to her boyfriend.
C. She returned it to the owner.
D. She turned it into a piece of furniture.

3. Who was Antonio Stradivari?

A. The lead cellist of an orchestra in Los Angeles
B. Melanie Stevens' boyfriend
C. Han-na Chang's teacher
D. A great cello maker

4. When did people begin to make mass-produced cellos?

A. In 1684
B. In 1757
C. In the nineteenth century
D. In the twentieth century

INFERENCE

5. Why did wealthy people buy old cellos?

A. To sell them later at a higher price
B. To give them to great musicians
C. To turn them into cabinets
D. To play beautiful music

TEXT REFERENCE

6. In line 17, *Today they are worth millions*, what does the word *they* refer to?

A. Mass-produced cellos
B. Wealthy people
C. Cello makers
D. Old cellos

VOCABULARY REVIEW

MYSTERY PHRASE

Fill in the blanks. Then unscramble the letters in the circles to complete the mystery phrase.

1. A violin is kept in a [ ][a][ ][○].
2. A person who writes music is a [c][ ][m][○][o][s][ ][ ].
3. Tell a [j][○][ ][ ] to make someone laugh.
4. The cello is an instrument in a classical [ ][○][c][ ][ ][s][t][ ][a].
5. Some people are born with [○][ ][l][e][ ][t]. They are naturally musical.
6. The [c][ ][○][d][ ][ ][t][ ][r] stands between the audience and the orchestra.
7. A [c][ ][b][○][n][ ][ ] is a good place to store CDs.
8. We were [a][s][ ][ ][u][○][d][ ][d] by the acoustics in the new building. The concert sounded great.
9. Make the right [ ][n][v][ ][ ][t][○][ ][n][t] and you will be wealthy someday.

Mystery phrase:

Mozart was a [○][○][○][○][○][○][○][○][○] composer.

WORDS IN CONTEXT

Fill in the blanks with words from each box.

acoustics	significant	stolen	move	economical

1. I love music and often go to concerts. Music is very _______ in my life.
2. Front row tickets are too expensive. Let's buy more _______ tickets.
3. The police found my _______ wallet on the bus.
4. This hall has great _______. Concerts here always sound wonderful.
5. We plan to _______ soon because this house is too small.

lead	wandered	hold	highlight	crafted

6. The _______ of Tom's career was winning first prize in the world cello competition.
7. Sue's hobby is making furniture. She _______ this table by hand.
8. We _______ around the city all day and saw many interesting things.
9. After years of playing in the orchestra, Ms. Oh finally became the _______ cellist.
10. That shelf is too small to _______ all my books.

individually	privilege	spied	takes	arrange

11. It ________ a lot of hard work to become an excellent musician.

12. The teacher spoke to each student ________.

13. When I ________ that beautiful sweater in the store, I knew I had to buy it.

14. I'll ________ my schedule to make time for music lessons.

15. It was a great ________ to meet that famous musician.

WORD FAMILIES

Fill in the blanks with words from each box.

composer (*noun*)	**compositions** (*noun*)	**composed** (*verb*)

1. I always enjoy ________ by Mozart.

2. He ________ a lot of beautiful music.

prominence (*noun*)	**prominent** (*adjective*)	**prominently** (*adverb*)

3. Because of her ________, she was invited to perform at Carnegie Hall.

4. Han-na Chang is a ________ cellist.

superbness (*noun*)	**superb** (*adjective*)	**superbly** (*adverb*)

5. The orchestra performed ________ last night.

6. I think they are ________ musicians.

WRONG WORD

One word in each group does not fit. Circle the word.

1. cello	violin	conductor	piano
2. enormous	small	tiny	little
3. cabinet	table	sofa	window
4. wander	sit	walk	travel
5. philosophy	history	school	mathematics
6. superb	excellent	wonderful	dreadful

SENTENCE COMPLETION

Complete the letter with words from the box.

philosophy superb worth interfere orchestra truly

To: Bob
From: Laura
Subject: concert tickets

Bob,

Great news! I have tickets for Carnegie Hall tonight. If you want to hear a great _______ play, come with me. These tickets are _______ $75, but I got them for free. I promise you the performance will be _______. They are _______ excellent musicians. I know you're busy studying for your _______ class, but don't worry. We'll get home early, so this won't _______ with your schedule. I hope you can come. Let me know soon.

Laura

WHAT ABOUT YOU?

Speaking

Ask your partner these questions.

1. Who in your family likes to tell jokes?
2. What is something that you keep in a case?
3. Who is your favorite composer?
4. Who is significant in your life?
5. What is one of your talents?

Writing

Now write about your partner. Use your partner's answers to the questions.

Example: Annie's uncle likes to tell jokes.

1. ______________________________
2. ______________________________
3. ______________________________
4. ______________________________
5. ______________________________

READING QUIZ

Read the passage and answer the questions. Circle your answers.

 TALENTED CONDUCTOR WANTED 

We are looking for someone to lead a superb group of musicians.

Who we are: The Tiny Tims are a small group of teenage violin and cello players with an enormous amount of talent!

What we do: We play free concerts for audiences who don't have enough money to go to the orchestra.

What we play: Music from many famous composers (mainly from the 18th century)

When we practice: Every Monday night at 7 P.M. (unless it interferes with a concert by the senior Philharmonic orchestra). We also practice individually.

Last year's highlights: Our group was on a TV talent show for teenagers in Tokyo. We were ranked 14th in Asia. One of our cellos was stolen at the airport, and our story was reported on the news. A wealthy man heard about us and arranged for us to come and play at his birthday party. All of his guests were homeless people. As a gift, he gave us each a ticket to Tokyo Disneyland.

Our philosophy: Orchestra music is for everyone, not just the wealthy and privileged.

We are a dedicated group, but we also like to tell jokes and have fun. Please e-mail Toshi at **tinytims@curio-city.com** if you are interested in being our conductor.

MAIN IDEA

1. What is this advertisement for?

A. Free concerts
B. A trip to Disneyland
C. A job for a conductor
D. Lessons for young musicians

DETAIL

2. Who are The Tiny Tims?

A. A small orchestra
B. A music school
C. A TV program
D. A concert hall

3. What did a wealthy man do?

A. He stole a cello.
B. He reported the news.
C. He appeared on a TV talent show.
D. He invited homeless people to a party.

INFERENCE

4. What kind of music do The Tiny Tims play?

A. Classical
B. Piano
C. Modern
D. Guitar

VOCABULARY

5. What does *individually* in line 15 mean?

A. Together
B. Everyday
C. One by one
D. On a schedule

6. What does *stolen* in line 19 mean?

A. Bought
B. Played
C. Taken
D. Noticed

UNIT 8 NEW YEAR

PEOPLE

PREPARE TO READ

Discuss these questions.

1. Look at the chart. What animal represents the year you were born?
2. Do you believe our time of birth can affect our personalities?

WORD FOCUS

Match the words with their definitions.

A.

1. according to __	a. loving
2. affectionate __	b. kind; giving
3. generous __	c. affect
4. horoscope __	d. as said by
5. influence __	e. a system of telling a person's future based on their time of birth

B.

1. loyal __	a. interested in love
2. pessimistic __	b. having negative thoughts
3. romantic __	c. dependable as a friend
4. sincere __	d. honest
5. stubborn __	e. not wanting to change

SCAN

A. Guess the answer. Circle *a* or *b*.

How many animals are there in the Chinese horoscope?

a. Ten ***b.*** Twelve

B. Scan the passage quickly to check your answer.

TRACK 23

THE CHINESE HOROSCOPE AND YOUR PERSONALITY

What kind of person are you? Are you friendly or shy? Maybe you're **romantic**. You might be artistic. Where does your personality come from? Many people believe that your time of birth **influences** your personality. The Chinese **horoscope** is one tradition that connects your personality with the year of your birth.

According to the Chinese horoscope, each year is represented by a different animal. There are twelve animals in the horoscope, and they repeat every twelve years. For example, the year 2000 was the year of the dragon, and the year 2012 will be the year of the dragon again. In order after the dragon, the next animals on the calendar are the snake, the horse, the sheep, the monkey, the rooster, the dog, the pig, the rat, the ox, the tiger, and the rabbit.

These horoscope animals influence the personality of someone born that year. Were you born in 1983? That was the year of the pig. You are honest and **affectionate**. Were you born in 1982, the year of the dog? Then you are hardworking, but also a little **pessimistic**. If you were born in 1984, the year of the rat, you are charming and **generous**. If you were born in 1985, the year of the ox, you are calm, **sincere**, and **stubborn**. 1986 was the year of the tiger. Tigers have a good attitude toward life and are **loyal** to their friends.

Are you honest like a pig or generous like a rat? Are you stubborn like an ox or quiet like a rabbit? Perhaps the animal of your year has an influence on you.

WHICH MEANING?

What does *kind* mean in line 1?

1 (*noun*) type
2 (*adjective*) helpful
3 (*adjective*) patient

CHECK YOUR COMPREHENSION

Read the passage again and answer the questions. Circle your answers.

MAIN IDEA

1. What is this passage mainly about?

A. Different kinds of animals
B. Good and bad friends
C. A traditional belief
D. Animal caretakers

DETAIL

2. Which of the following animals is NOT on the Chinese horoscope?

A. Rat
B. Pig
C. Dog
D. Cat

3. Which words describe people born in the year of the ox?

A. Calm and honest
B. Dependable and loyal
C. Charming and giving
D. Hardworking and negative

4. When was the year of the tiger?

A. 1983
B. 1984
C. 1985
D. 1986

INFERENCE

5. 1988 was the year of which animal?

A. The snake
B. The horse
C. The sheep
D. The dragon

TEXT ORGANIZATION

6. Which paragraph lists the names of all the animals on the horoscope?

A. The first paragraph
B. The second paragraph
C. The third paragraph
D. The fourth paragraph

PLACES

PREPARE TO READ

Discuss these questions.

1. What is happening in the photo? Do you know any other famous New Year's Eve celebrations?
2. Where do you like to spend New Year's Eve? What do you do ten seconds before the New Year arrives?

WORD FOCUS

Match the words with their definitions.

A.

1. approach __ a. go down
2. balloon __ b. small pieces of colored paper
3. celebration __ c. come near
4. confetti __ d. a party to mark a special event or day
5. descend __ e. a colored bag filled with air

B.

1. distribute __ a. amazing
2. lower __ b. the sound a clock makes
3. sparkle __ c. drop
4. spectacular __ d. give to many people
5. tick __ e. shine

SCAN

A. Guess the answer. Circle *a* or *b*.

When did the first New Year's celebration occur in Times Square?

a. 1904 ***b.*** 1994

B. Scan the passage quickly to check your answer.

TRACK 24

New Year's Eve in Times Square

You may have seen this on television. Despite the chilly winter weather, thousands of people head for Times Square in New York City on the evening of December 31. They stand for hours in the cold night air watching the clock. The crowd grows larger as the hours **tick** by. People walk around **distributing balloons**, flags, and **confetti**. Soon music begins playing, and everyone sings along. Midnight **approaches**, and the crowd becomes more and more excited. At 11:59, an enormous lighted ball starts **descending** a flagpole. Everyone counts as it nears the bottom. Five. . .four. . .three. . .two. . .one. . .Happy New Year! Thousands of voices cheer as the ball reaches the bottom of the pole and fireworks light up the sky. People hug and kiss each other and wave at the TV cameras. Confetti and balloons fill the air.

The New Year's **celebration** in Times Square is an old tradition. The first one occurred in 1904. Nowadays, TV has also become part of the tradition. Many families across the United States gather in their living rooms to watch the lighted ball descend the flagpole at midnight. The first New Year's ball was **lowered** down a flagpole in 1907. That ball was made of iron and wood and weighed over 300 kilos. It was decorated with 100 light bulbs. The ball that is used now is covered with glass, mirrors, and hundreds of colored lights. It **sparkles** and shines **spectacularly** as it goes down the pole to welcome the New Year.

WHICH MEANING?

What does *wave* mean in line 10?

1 (*noun*) a curl in the hair
2 (*verb*) move the hand in greeting
3 (*noun*) motion of water

CHECK YOUR COMPREHENSION

Read the passage again and answer the questions. Circle your answers.

MAIN IDEA

1. What is this passage mainly about?
   - **A.** A yearly celebration
   - **B.** A visit to New York
   - **C.** A TV show
   - **D.** A concert

DETAIL

2. What can you see in Times Square on December 31?
   - **A.** People singing
   - **B.** Balloons and confetti
   - **C.** A large, lighted ball
   - **D.** All of the above

3. What do people do in Times Square when midnight arrives?
   - **A.** They wave and cheer.
   - **B.** They play a ball game.
   - **C.** They turn on their TVs.
   - **D.** They look in the mirror.

4. How much did the first New Year's ball weigh?
   - **A.** Over 100 kilos
   - **B.** 190 kilos
   - **C.** Over 300 kilos
   - **D.** 1,907 kilos

INFERENCE

5. How long does it take the New Year's ball to descend the flagpole?
   - **A.** Five seconds
   - **B.** One minute
   - **C.** Five minutes
   - **D.** One hour

TEXT REFERENCE

6. In line 7, *Everyone counts as it nears the bottom*, what does the word *it* refer to?
   - **A.** The ball
   - **B.** The clock
   - **C.** The crowd
   - **D.** The flagpole

THINGS

PREPARE TO READ

Discuss these questions.

1. How do you dress on New Year's Day?
2. What other things do you do to celebrate the New Year?

WORD FOCUS

Match the words with their definitions.

A.

1. fortune __	**a.** something you do often
2. fresh __	**b.** related to the moon
3. habit __	**c.** a matched set of clothes
4. lunar __	**d.** luck
5. outfit __	**e.** new

A.

1. pine __	**a.** hit
2. precisely __	**b.** greet
3. strike __	**c.** a kind of tree
4. welcome __	**d.** exactly
5. whistle __	**e.** a toy that sounds like a bird when you blow air through it

SCAN

A. Guess if this is true or false. Circle *a* or *b*.

People in Mexico wear red underwear to welcome the New Year.

a. True ***b.*** False

B. Scan the passage quickly to check your answer.

TRACK 25

Celebrating the New Year

In some places, people celebrate New Year's Day on January first. In other places, they celebrate the **lunar** New Year. But in every place, people like to **welcome** the New Year in special ways.

In many Asian countries, children get gifts of money on New Year's Day. The money is inside special red envelopes. These gifts bring the children good **fortune** and happiness. People also like to decorate their houses for the New Year. In China, red is the color of good luck, so many of the decorations are red. In Japan, people decorate their houses with **pine** branches, rope, and bamboo. These things are symbols of good health and long life.

Clothes are part of many New Year's celebrations. In China, children wear new **outfits** on New Year's Day. In Korea and Japan, many people put on traditional clothes for the holiday. In South America, people wear yellow underwear for good luck. In Mexico, some people wear red underwear to bring romance in the New Year.

In Spain, people welcome the New Year with grapes. **Precisely** when the clock **strikes** midnight, they eat twelve grapes. They try to swallow them all rapidly before the clock finishes striking twelve. In North America, people welcome the New Year with a lot of noise. At midnight, they use horns and **whistles** to make as much noise as they can.

People everywhere enjoy celebrating the New Year. It's a time to make a **fresh** start, change bad **habits**, and look forward to a future of happiness and good luck.

WHICH MEANING?
What does *horns* mean in line 17?

1 (*noun*) pieces of bone on an animal's head
2 (*noun*) musical instruments
3 (*noun*) toys that makes a lot of noise

CHECK YOUR COMPREHENSION

Read the passage again and answer the questions. Circle your answers.

MAIN IDEA

1. What is this passage mainly about?

A. New Year's gifts
B. The lunar New Year
C. Clothes for the New Year
D. New Year's traditions

DETAIL

2. In ________, people use pine branches as decorations to celebrate the New Year.

A. China
B. Korea
C. Japan
D. Mexico

3. Why do some people wear yellow underwear to celebrate the New Year?

A. For money
B. For good luck
C. For health and long life
D. For romance and happiness

4. How do people in North America celebrate the New Year?

A. They eat special food.
B. They make a lot of noise.
C. They wear special clothes.
D. They decorate their houses.

INFERENCE

5. People everywhere

A. want good fortune in the New Year.
B. believe that red means good luck.
C. stay home on New Year's Day.
D. eat grapes at midnight.

TEXT ORGANIZATION

6. Which paragraph mentions a Korean New Year's tradition?

A. The first paragraph
B. The second paragraph
C. The third paragraph
D. The fourth paragraph

VOCABULARY REVIEW

CROSSWORD PUZZLE

Complete the crossword using the clues.

Across

1. exactly
2. biting your nails is a bad one
8. describes a fireworks display
9. tiny pieces of paper to throw

Down

1. describes a person with a negative attitude
3. It sounds like a bird when you blow through it.
4. the sound of a second on a clock
5. your future and fortune according to your time of birth
6. a colored bag of air for a celebration
7. a matched set of clothes to wear

WORDS IN CONTEXT

Fill in the blanks with words from each box.

according to	descends	strikes	sparkles	romantic

1. This elevator _______ very slowly. It's faster to go down the stairs.
2. My boyfriend is so _______. He always brings me flowers.
3. He also gave me a huge diamond ring that really _______.
4. When the clock _______ twelve, we'll have to go home.
5. _______ the Chinese horoscope, I was born in the year of the sheep.

lower	lunar	distribute	fortune	loyal

6. We plan to _______ balloons to everyone at the party.
7. According to the _______ calendar, the New Year is in February.
8. I can always depend on Shirley. She's a very _______ friend.
9. When they _______ the New Year's ball in Times Square, it's exciting!
10. I've had really bad luck this year, so I hope for good _______ next year.

horn	pine	approached	celebration	waved

11. I love parties, and I always have a big _______ on my birthday.
12. When midnight arrived, everyone blew his or her _______ loudly.
13. The hills were covered with _______ trees.
14. We _______ good-bye as the train left the station.
15. As we _______ the beach, we could feel the ocean breeze.

WORD FAMILIES

Fill in the blanks with words from each box.

influence (*noun*)	**influences** (*verb*)	**influential** (*adjective*)

1. My parents are very _______ in my life.
2. My brother also _______ me a lot.

romance (*noun*)	**romantic** (*adjective*)	**romantically** (*adverb*)

3. I like movies that are about _______.
4. This music is very _______.

fortune (*noun*)	**fortunate** (*adjective*)	**fortunately** (*adverb*)

5. Roger has a nice family and a lot of friends. He's a very _______ person.
6. _______, I was close to home when it started to rain.

TRUE OR FALSE?

Are the following sentences true or false? Circle your answers.

1. A whistle makes a sound like a bird.	TRUE	FALSE
2. Generous people like to share.	TRUE	FALSE
3. Pessimistic people have a positive attitude.	TRUE	FALSE
4. Sincere people often tell lies.	TRUE	FALSE
5. When you welcome someone, you say "good-bye."	TRUE	FALSE
6. Fresh fruit is old.	TRUE	FALSE
7. Affectionate people show a lot of love.	TRUE	FALSE
8. Stubborn people change their minds easily.	TRUE	FALSE

SENTENCE COMPLETION

Complete the postcard with words from the box.

confetti	fortune	celebration	kinds	outfit	struck

Hi Jack,

I'm having a fantastic vacation! I went to a great New Year's ______ last night. It was a really fun party. I looked very nice— I wore my new ______. The food was excellent. We had different ______ of sandwiches and cake. When the clock ______ midnight, everyone threw ______ in the air. It was so much fun.

I wish you a happy New Year, and I hope you have lots of good ______ this year.

Love,

Sally

WHAT ABOUT YOU?

Speaking

Ask your partner these questions.

1. What do you usually do at your birthday celebration?
2. What kinds of music do you like?
3. Who influences you?
4. What is one of your bad habits?
5. What kind of outfit do you wear to celebrate the New Year?

Writing

Now write about your partner. Use your partner's answers to the questions.

Example: Dave usually eats cake and dances at his birthday celebration.

1. ______________________________
2. ______________________________
3. ______________________________
4. ______________________________
5. ______________________________

READING QUIZ

Read the passage and answer the questions. Circle your answers.

Teen Whiz Survey

At precisely 12:00 A.M., on January 1, teenagers around the world will welcome another New Year. Many teens make a resolution for the New Year. Last month, *Teen Whiz* magazine asked readers to answer this question: What is your #1 resolution for the New Year? The results are in the chart below.

New Year's Resolutions	% of our readers	Words from our readers...
Get a fresh appearance	30%	"I'm going to buy a new outfit for my birthday celebration!" —Yolanda
Stop a bad habit	20%	"I always whistle while I work. I have to stop!" —Luc
Be more affectionate	10%	"I want to show my boyfriend I can be romantic." —Sherry
Be more generous	10%	"I want to share my good fortune with others." —Franz
Change my attitude	5%	"I am too pessimistic about life. I want to be happy every day." —Maria
Read my horoscope	2%	"I want to meet someone who was born in the year of the dragon." —Mia
Other	23%	"I need to be more loyal to my friends." —Joey

The clock is ticking.... Do you have a New Year's resolution yet?

MAIN IDEA

1. What is this article mainly about?

A. People with good habits
B. Reasons why people read a magazine
C. Teenagers' plans for improving their lives
D. Teenagers' plans for celebrating a holiday

DETAIL

2. Who has a bad habit?

A. Sherry
B. Luc
C. Yolanda
D. Maria

3. How many readers want to change their appearance?

A. 5%
B. 10%
C. 20%
D. 30%

INFERENCE

4. What is probably true about Maria?

A. She often feels lucky.
B. She is a positive person.
C. She is happy most of the time.
D. She usually has a negative attitude.

VOCABULARY

5. What does *welcome* in line 1 mean?

A. Greet
B. Celebrate
C. Spend
D. Enjoy

6. What does *fortune* in line 10 mean?

A. Possessions
B. Friendships
C. Luck
D. Time

VOCABULARY SELF-QUIZ

You can use these word lists to quiz yourself.

1. First, write your translations next to the English words. Study them for a while.
2. Then, quiz yourself. Cover up the English words. You should only look at your translations.
3. Try to remember the English words and write them down. How many words can you remember?

Unit 1 STUNTS

PEOPLE	TRANSLATION	TEST YOURSELF
contest		
dream		
fascinate		
injure		
instead		
kick		
punch		
star		
stunt		
teenager		

PLACES		
acrobatics		
applicant		
course		
enroll		
martial arts		
mentally		
physically		
require		
train		
trousers		

THINGS		
audience		
brave		
explode		
flame		
pretend		
protect		
risky		
shoot		
spin		
turn over		

Unit 2 COLOR

PEOPLE	TRANSLATION	TEST YOURSELF
colorful		
condition		
experience		
form		
report		
sense		
separate		
smooth		
strange		
triangle		

PLACES		
bright		
death		
dull		
grab		
iguana		
poison		
predator		
prey		
squeeze		
warn		

THINGS		
affect		
beige		
calm		
decorate		
encourage		
mood		
negative		
positive		
public		
refreshing		

Unit 3 CIRCUS

PEOPLE	TRANSLATION	TEST YOURSELF
accomplishment		
balance		
concentration		
juggle		
native		
original		
patience		
perseverance		
professional		
tie in		

PLACES		
caretaker		
coach		
entire		
equipment		
head		
load		
pull into		
snack		
sore		
unload		

THINGS		
attitude		
community		
cultural		
effort		
emperor		
festival		
generation		
impact		
look down upon		
village		

Unit 4 SHARKS

PEOPLE	TRANSLATION	TEST YOURSELF
aquarium		
college		
creature		
dedicate		
degree		
dive		
inhabit		
knowledge		
occur		
shark		

PLACES		
aggressive		
agriculture		
coast		
coral		
disappear		
fin		
marine		
pollution		
reef		
treasure		

THINGS		
birth		
come across		
dare		
gigantic		
jaw		
nutrition		
replace		
solitary		
swallow		
wear down		

Unit 5 SPORTS

PEOPLE	TRANSLATION	TEST YOURSELF
attempt		
career		
cemetery		
coach		
emphasize		
overcome		
qualify		
rapid		
success		
tough		

PLACES		
boundaries		
citizen		
combine		
extreme		
gather		
huge		
set out		
spread		
surface		
tow		

THINGS		
develop		
innocence		
rank		
represent		
respect		
ripen		
root		
symbolize		
treat		
wisdom		

Unit 6 MONSTERS

PEOPLE	TRANSLATION	TEST YOURSELF
coffin		
devil		
dragon		
evil		
identify		
myth		
reflection		
superstitious		
vampire		
victim		

PLACES

century		
chilly		
claim		
evidence		
exist		
hoax		
investigate		
legend		
resemble		
turn out		

THINGS

advice		
associate		
average		
charm		
dreadful		
god		
powerful		
prevent		
reptile		
wound		

Unit 7 MUSIC

PEOPLE	TRANSLATION	TEST YOURSELF
arrange		
astounded		
cello		
conductor		
enormous		
interfere		
orchestra		
philosophy		
significant		
talent		

PLACES		
acoustics		
case		
composer		
highlight		
joke		
privilege		
prominent		
superb		
truly		
wander		

THINGS		
cabinet		
craft		
economical		
individually		
investment		
lead		
mass-produced		
spy		
stolen		
worth		

Unit 8 NEW YEAR

PEOPLE	TRANSLATION	TEST YOURSELF
according to		
affectionate		
generous		
horoscope		
influence		
loyal		
pessimistic		
romantic		
sincere		
stubborn		

PLACES		
approach		
balloon		
celebration		
confetti		
descend		
distribute		
lower		
sparkle		
spectacular		
tick		

THINGS		
fortune		
fresh		
habit		
lunar		
outfit		
pine		
precisely		
strike		
welcome		
whistle		

VOCABULARY INDEX

The number refers to the page where the word appears in the reading passages.

A

accomplishment **23**, 47
according to **73**
acoustics **65**
acrobatics **5**, 11, 23, 27
(acrobat 25, 31)
advice **57**, 61
affect **17**
affectionate **73**, 81
aggressive **35**, 37, 41
agriculture **35**
applicant **5**, 11
approach **75**
aquarium **33**, 41
arrange **63**, 71
associate **57**, 61, 63
astounded **63**
attempt **43**, 45, 51
attitude **27**, 73, 81
audience **7**, 11, 23, 31, 63, 71
average **57**, 61

B

balance **23**, 31
balloon **75**
beige **17**
birth **37**, 41, 73
boundaries **45**
brave **7**
bright **15**, 17, 21

C

cabinet **67**
calm **17**, 21, 73
career **43**, 51, 65
caretaker **25**
case **65**
celebration **75**, 77, 81
cello **63**, 67, 71
cemetery **43**
century **55**, 67, 71
charm **57**, 73
chilly **55**, 61, 75
citizen **45**
claim **55**
coach (passenger car) **25**, 31
coach (sports trainer) **43**, 51
coast **35**, 45
coffin **53**, 61
college **33**, 41
colorful **13**, 15, 45
combine **45**, 51
(combination **47**)
come across **37**, 41, 53
community **27**, 31
composer **65**, 71
concentration **23**, 31, 43, 51
condition **13**
conductor **63**, 71
confetti **75**
contest **3**, 11
coral **35**, 41
course **5**, 11
craft **67**
creature **33**, 37, 41, 57, 61
cultural **27**

D

dare **37**, 41
death **15**, 21
decorate **17**, 75, 77
dedicate **33**, 41, 71
(dedication 43, 65)
degree **33**, 41
descend **75**
develop **47**
devil **53**, 61
disappear **35**, 37
distribute **75**
dive **33**, 35, 41
dragon **53**, 57, 61, 73, 81
dreadful **57**, 61
dream **3**, 11, 21, 23, 31, 51
dull **15**, 21

E

economical **67**
effort **27**, 31
emperor **27**, 31, 57
emphasize **43**, 51
encourage **17**, 21
enormous **63**, 71, 75
enroll **5**, 11, 23, 31
entire **25**, 27, 31, 43
equipment **25**, 27, 31
evidence **55**
evil **53**, 57, 61
exist **55**
experience **13**, 17, 21
explode **7**
extreme **45**, 51
(extremely 63)

F

fascinate **3**, 11, 33
festival **27**, 31
fin **35**, 37, 41
flame **7**
form **13**, 27
fortune **77**, 81
fresh **77**, 81

G

gather **45**, 51, 75
generation **27**
generous **73**, 81
gigantic **37**, 41, 55, 57
god **57**
grab **15**, 31, 37

H

habit **77**, 81
head **25**, 75
highlight **65**, 71
hoax **55**
horoscope **73**, 81
huge **45**, 63

I

identify **53**, 55, 61
iguana **15**
impact **27**
individually **67**, 71
influence **73**
inhabit **33**, 35, 41
injure **3**, 7, 11, 35, 51
(injury 41)
innocence **47**
instead **3**, 27, 37, 43, 67
interfere **63**, 71
investigate **55**
(investigator 61)
investment **67**

J

jaw **37**, 41
joke **65**, 71
juggle **23**, 27, 31

K
kick **3**, 7, 11
knowledge **33**, 41, 47

L
lead **67**, 71
legend **55**
load **25**
look down upon **27**
lower **75**
loyal **73**, 81
lunar **77**

M
marine **35**, 37, 41
martial arts **5**, 11
mass-produced **67**
mentally **5**, 11
(mental 51)
mood **17**
myth **53**, 57, 61

N
native **23**, 63
negative **17**, 21
nutrition **37**

O
occur **33**, 41, 75
orchestra **63**, 67, 71
original **23**, 31
outfit **77**, 81
overcome **43**, 51

P
patience **23**
perseverance **23**
pessimistic **73**, 81
philosophy **63**, 71
physically **5**, 11
(physical 51)
pine **77**
poison **15**
(poisonous 15, 35)
pollution **35**
positive **17**, 21
powerful **57**
precisely **77**, 81
predator **15**, 37, 41
pretend **7**, 11
prevent **57**, 61
prey **15**, 37
privilege **65**, 71
professional **23**, 27, 31, 41, 43, 45, 51
prominent **65**, 67
protect **7**, 11, 15, 35, 53, 57
public **17**
pull into **25**, 31
punch **3**, 7, 11

Q
qualify **43**, 51

R
rank **47**, 51, 71
rapid **43**, 45, 51, 77
reef **35**, 41
reflection **53**, 61
refreshing **17**, 21
replace **37**
report **13**, 21, 55, 67, 71
represent **47**, 57, 73
reptile **57**
require **5**, 11, 43
resemble **55**, 57
respect **47**, 57
ripen **47**
risky **7**, 11, 41
(risks 27)
romantic **73**, 81
(romance 77)
root **47**, 51

S
sense **13**
separate **13**, 25, 31, 35, 41
set out **45**, 51
shark **33**, 35, 37, 41
shoot **7**
significant **63**
sincere **73**
smooth **13**
snack **25**, 31
solitary **37**, 53
sore **25**, 31
sparkle **75**
spectacular **75**
spin **7**, 11
spread **45**, 51
spy **67**
squeeze **15**, 23, 31
star **3**, 11
stolen **67**, 71
strange **13**, 55
strike **77**
stubborn **73**
stunt **3**, 5, 7, 11
success **43**
superb **65**, 71
superstitious **53**, 55, 57
(superstitions 61)
surface **45**
swallow **37**, 77
symbolize **47**, 65
(symbol 57, 77)

T
talent **63**, 65, 71
teenager **3**, 11, 51, 71, 81
tick **75**, 81
tie in **23**
tough **43**, 51
tow **45**
train **5**, 7, 11, 23, 27, 33, 41, 43
(trainer 25)
treasure **35**
treat **47**, 57
triangle **13**
trousers **5**
truly **65**
turn out **55**, 61
turn over **7**

U
unload **25**, 31

V
vampire **53**, 61
victim **53**, 61
village **27**, 31

W
wander **65**
warn **15**, 21
(warning 47)
wear down **37**
welcome **77**, 81
whistle **77**, 81
wisdom **47**
(wise 57)
worth **67**
wound **57**, 61

COMMON IRREGULAR VERBS

INFINITIVE	SIMPLE PAST	PAST PARTICIPLE
be	was/were	been
become	became	become
begin	began	begun
bite	bit	bitten
blow	blew	blown
break	broke	broken
bring	brought	brought
build	built	built
burn	burned/burnt	burned/burnt
buy	bought	bought
catch	caught	caught
choose	chose	chosen
come	came	come
cost	cost	cost
cut	cut	cut
dive	dived/dove	dived
do	did	done
draw	drew	drawn
dream	dreamed/dreamt	dreamed/dreamt
drink	drank	drunk
drive	drove	driven
eat	ate	eaten
fall	fell	fallen
feel	felt	felt
fight	fought	fought
find	found	found
fit	fit/fitted	fit/fitted
fly	flew	flown
forbid	forbade	forbidden
get	got	gotten
give	gave	given
go	went	gone/been
grow	grew	grown
hang	hung	hung
have	had	had
hear	heard	heard
hide	hid	hidden
hit	hit	hit
hold	held	held
hurt	hurt	hurt
keep	kept	kept
know	knew	known
leave	left	left

INFINITIVE	SIMPLE PAST	PAST PARTICIPLE
let	let	let
light	lit/lighted	lit/lighted
lose	lost	lost
make	made	made
mean	meant	meant
meet	met	met
overcome	overcame	overcome
pay	paid	paid
put	put	put
read	read	read
ride	rode	ridden
rise	rose	risen
run	ran	run
say	said	said
see	saw	seen
sell	sold	sold
set	set	set
shoot	shot	shot
show	showed	shown
sing	sang	sung
sit	sat	sat
sleep	slept	slept
speak	spoke	spoken
speed	sped	sped
spend	spent	spent
spread	spread	spread
stand	stood	stood
steal	stole	stolen
strike	struck	struck/stricken
swim	swam	swum
take	took	taken
teach	taught	taught
tear	tore	torn
tell	told	told
think	thought	thought
throw	threw	thrown
understand	understood	understood
wake	woke	woken
wear	wore	worn
win	won	won
write	wrote	written